Leadership Transition Coaching

Leadership Transition Coaching

*Mary Valette Devine and
Inge Nieuwstraten*

Open University Press

Open University Press
McGraw Hill
8th Floor, 338 Euston Road
London
England
NW1 3BH

email: enquiries@openup.co.uk
world wide web: www.openup.co.uk

First edition published 2021

A catalogue record of this book is available from the British Library

ISBN-13: 9780335250332
ISBN-10: 0335250335
eISBN: 9780335250349

Library of Congress Cataloging-in-Publication Data
CIP data applied for

Typeset by Transforma Pvt. Ltd., Chennai, India

Praise page

As a former Military Officer in the Irish Defense Forces and now a Chartered Work Psychologist, I have had a long-standing interest in Leadership theory. However, my core question for leaders has always been; "how do you practice leadership?" This book is very welcome and timely in that it provides an excellent space for the leader / coach to deeply reflect on and consider the values, goals and behaviors that underpin the onerous responsibility and practice of leading others at a time where the very sustainability of our global system is under threat.
Hugh O'Donovan CPsychol., P.s.S.I, Coaching / Work Psychologist, Co-Founder of the 1ˢᵗ Masters in Coaching Psychology in an Irish University (UCC), and Author of Mindful Walking

Leadership Transition Coaching comes at an opportune time for all leaders given the current volatile and complex nature of our world. This is an excellent book with academic rigour and practical insight into the struggle and response of leaders as they address the challenges of the workplace today. This text not only deepens practice but also facilitates rich reflection on what it is to be a leader and how best to navigate transitions effectively in collaboration with others.
Pat O'Leary, Director MSc in Personal and Management Coaching, University College Cork, Ireland

Drawing on existing coaching theory and new research on the impact of coaching, this useful book is a valuable roadmap for leaders in transition. As an executive coach working with clients at different phases of life, I found the book relevant and practical. I will be using it in my practice.
Pamela Fay, Executive Coach, Coach Supervisor and Coach Tutor, www.pamelafay.ie

This book is a fabulous resource, not just for coaches and trainers of coaches, but for anyone who is navigating the changes which present themselves when we step into a leadership position. It provides fresh insights into how coaching can support leaders in transition and the case studies, in particular, bring the material to life. The link the authors have made to the importance of coaching for new leaders as they navigate the challenges they encounter, both cognitively and emotionally in their new role, is clearly and intelligently presented. This is a timely and highly relevant book for the coaching community.
Paula King, MSc Coaching; Master Coach EMCC/ICF

Contents

Introduction

Mary Valette Devine

This book has been written out of a curiosity to understand how a leader crosses the bridge of change into a new role and how they hold their confidence and bring the best of themselves to the role. Leaders have a lot of influence on the teams they lead, the organizations they serve as well as on the wider society. Coaches are often the trusted agent whose confidential support leaders lean on as they make their transition into new territory. Even though leaders can have held many leadership roles before, every new position with its own sense of time in the world is uniquely different.

Consider how ways of working have changed: both the ways and places of working have shifted from a local to a national and now into a global context. Virtual working has accelerated at a huge pace. These changing scenarios, complete with generational diversity, call for leadership that can meet the expectations of our current time in the world.

So, what are some of the real challenges and opportunities leaders can encounter? What can be the true impact of coaching if the leader engages with a coach as she or he transitions to a new role? What are the key areas these leaders are likely to see as important during those first few weeks and months as they navigate at this unique time of personal change? Why is the leader's perspective so valuable for coaches in leadership transition? Welcome to Leadership Transition Coaching.

Leaders show up with different beliefs, values and, ultimately, behaviours. Sometimes, these behaviours do not always encourage followership of the leader both from within the company or from external stakeholders. Hence the leader's role would become short-lived over time. Derailment is a risk for leaders and even more so in the complex and volatile time we live in.

Quick turnaround of leaders – especially at more senior levels – can leave organizations in flux for a while and is costly for both the individual and the organization. Leadership development programmes go some way to supporting leaders on their career journey within the organizations in which they lead.

In the past, leadership development programmes primarily focused on the delivery of streamlined development solutions, thus leading to a one-size-fits-all. In more recent years, the more experiential focus of development has led to solutions being more tailored to the individual learner and in this case the leader.

Along with virtual learning being available 24/7, technology has greatly enhanced access to availability of a wide range of learning materials and innovative solutions, which can often provide instant feedback as the learner engages with the learning medium. So, the learner's journey can be very focused and rewarding.

In more recent times and with the emergence of the global COVID-19 pandemic crisis in February 2020, the necessity for leaders, both in governments and organizations across the globe, to adapt very quickly and transition into new ways of working became an overnight requirement.

As the virus would rampantly escalate with transference across communities of people, mobility became restricted and social distancing became the new normal. Governments and nations need to prepare to deal with new pandemics that will arrive in the years ahead.

For now, businesses have responded where possible and technology has enabled some employees to work from home during those critical months. For the health care workers and other emergency services, their presence was required on the front line with patient care in hospitals and other essential services. So, leaders on the front line and leaders working from home had major unexpected transitions ahead of them, quite apart from the workers who have been furloughed.

Leadership transitions take many forms and while this book specifically takes a close look at leaders moving into new roles, transitions can also take place when organizational change happens and more recently when a pandemic health crisis looms across the globe.

So where does coaching fit in and what role do coaches play in the overall scope of leadership development? What is the impact of coaching for leaders as they navigate change, even more so at the time of transition? Having worked in the area of leadership development and coaching, it is useful to get an insight into why I would even consider writing a book on this topic.

Looking back to 2003, while working in a HR specialist role, I had a remit to support the introduction and embedding of performance management in a large company where leaders had strong technical capability. A key change that would need significant support was in the form of one-to-one interactions such as performance conversations between the individual leaders and their direct reports.

At that time, I searched to find a way forward that could support leaders to embrace the change and guide them in finding the best way to carry out that conversation. This was a step change from managing to leading, and new ways of thinking and acting would become a part of the change in behaviour that was needed.

I knew at that time that athletes had coaches to support them to reach the goals and performance levels to which they aspired. So, there was some psychology around coaching that had been getting good traction and maybe it could offer some insights to leaders who were meeting new challenges and ways of working.

My instincts guided me to understand that new behaviours would be at the forefront if performance management was to be successfully received and carried out within the organization. Coaching was introduced as part of the developmental pathway for those leaders back then. Initially, coaching was often perceived as a 'fix it' or remedial solution, rather than a progressive and sought-after development solution.

Some short years later, it got to the point where coaching was resourced both externally and internally. Some of the leaders became champions of coaching and pursued coaching qualifications, which allowed them to coach others within the business setting as required. Coaching was now evolving and with it came the development of policies and procedures that brought clarity, standards, ethics and supervision to coaching being undertaken.

Today, the coaching profession is still evolving and as a profession it offers accreditation levels that are recognized by the professional coaching bodies. Many leaders as they progress in their careers seek external coaches for reasons of confidentiality and for an external perspective. So, the strong influence of leaders and the impact of coaching have been uppermost in my mind even in the latter decades. Also, when return on investment is considered in the world of coaching, the voice of the leader who has been coached is recognized as a significant measure of the impact of coaching. This research makes those views accessible and is a further step in the evolution of coaching.

The opportunity to undertake research in Coaching Psychology and Positive Psychology at University College Cork, Ireland, allowed me to garner insights into the impact of coaching on leaders as they transition to a new role. This research has now been a cue for the writing of this book and it is timely with so much transition in a complex world to share what has found to be important for these leaders. Coaches are the trusted agents of these leaders at these critical junctures.

The book is intended to be a valuable resource for coaches or trainers of coaches whether they are working inside a company or externally with an educational body. It also provides insight for leaders who will be making transitions in the future and for those shaping development solutions for such leaders.

The Leadership Transition Coaching Framework is evidence based and built on the lived experience of leaders who were being coached at the unique time of transitioning to a new role. While coaches can use a range of techniques and frameworks in helping their clients' transition, the framework provided is not intended to be prescriptive. The information provides a resource for coaches as they choose what to take from their own varied toolkit.

The book:

- includes coaching questions that can be prompts for coaches as they consider what may be useful in the context they are working in;
- provides insight to leaders where specific topics may resonate as they reflect on the progress of their own transition;
- highlights commonalities in challenges faced by transitioning leaders;
- includes case studies drawn from real-life practice. All names and other identifying details have been changed to protect anonymity of individuals.

This book conveys the voices of eight leaders as they reflected on the impact of working with individual coaches as they navigated the transition into a new role. Their words convey their beliefs, values, emotions and truths that will be shared as openly as possible in this book. You may be a leader yourself or have coached leaders through a similar transition already. You may already have a good sense of what they experience.

The initial research I undertook for this project involved interviews with eight leaders, supervised by Inge Nieuwstraten at University College Cork. Further interviews were undertaken three years later and were held with leaders as they transitioned to C suite level. I also interviewed a new leader who was transitioning at the start of the pandemic COVID-19 virus. Confidentiality has been key to carrying out this research and all leaders mentioned throughout are under pseudonym names. The book provides a lens into the experience of eight senior leaders at their unique time of transition. Note quotes from their interviews in Chapter 5 are included to provide you with key insights about the overall experience of coaching. In addition, in an effort to show you how each of the themes are supported, it is necessary for some of the key quotes to be repeated in Chapters 7 to 10. The book brings a lens and a framework specific to Leadership Transition Coaching. It is a guide for coaches and trainers of coaches and provides insight too for leaders at times of transition. I hope the distilled deep knowledge and experience of the leaders that is captured in the book will be a useful resource for you in your work.

1 Leadership in an ever-changing world

In recent decades, much has been written on the topics of Leadership and Coaching both as individual topics and as topics that are mutually inclusive. The contexts are many and in this book the context is drawn from the authors' own research. The research focuses on the impact of coaching on leaders as they moved into a new role and how they experienced the coaching at this unique time of transition. The findings produce an evidence-based view and were the outcome of a study interviewing eight leaders who had been coached at a time when they were transitioning into a new role.

As technologies allow organizations to expand their work networks and are not limited by geographic locations, this opens up new opportunities for work. This weakens the notion of traditional workspaces where human connections brought a source of social engagement and personal support in closer face-to-face environments. In 2020 with a new wave of virtual working from homes and local places, neighbourhoods and communities are more important than ever and a new dependence on communities is deepening. The challenge for many leaders will be how they can adapt and lead teams while also collaborating with stakeholders in a virtual and global world.

Since the world of work is changing rapidly, the role of a new leader carries much influence and can be the making or breaking point within any setting. Within the organizational world, coaching is experiencing great growth and credibility in the field of leadership development. It is encouraging to see organizations invest in coaching, whether as a request from a new leader, or if it arrived as part of a leadership development programme. With this backdrop the authors sought to capture the characteristics of what truly was happening at a key time of transition for leaders on the move to a new role.

Others, too, have been asking similar questions. Coutu and Kauffman (2009) surveyed 140 leading coaches asking, 'What can coaching do for you?'. While, on this occasion, the survey participants were coaches instead of coaching clients, results indicated the top three reasons for engaging with a coach were 48 per cent to develop high potential or facilitate transition, 26 per cent to act as a sounding board and 12 per cent to address derailing behaviour.

Along with a global and complex environment, today in large developing economies such as China and India, leaders have often not long finished their studies and are getting their first wave of business experience just as they can arrive in a leadership role. Equally, new graduates arriving in companies may have leaders who are not much older than themselves and with limited leadership experience to match.

Coaching is likely to become a place of learning where the coach becomes a partner in the leaders' learning process, providing reflection, questioning and viewpoints that offer both challenge and support in critical areas. Equally, leaders can be transitioning to a role across the globe and can also be leading a multi-generational and a multi-cultural team.

In more recent years, the pace of organizational change, technological development, an intergenerational workforce and global economies were calling for adaptation at an accelerated rate. This environment brings the need for new ways of working, which calls for quick adaptation and significant resilience. What brought a leader success in the past is not a guarantee of bringing success in the future. As famously quoted, in the words of Marshall Goldsmith, 'What got you here won't get you there' (Goldsmith and Reiter 2013).

In 2010, Professor Lynda Gratton from London Business School collaborated with organizational thinkers and undertook research on the future of work (Gratton 2010). At that time, five areas emerged as important: the behaviours and actions of leaders were to become more scrutinized so their authenticity was key and in a more globally connected world they were called on to work in a more collaborative manner; they would need the capacity to lead and manage high-performing virtual teams; build networks both internally and externally and combine resources to create innovations; build valuable relationships with business partners, consumers and other entrepreneurial businesses; work with flexible work schedules while working across time zones.

Today, many leaders are encountering rapid change while navigating greater ambiguity and disruption. Now more than ever they will need to build collaborative partnerships and create trust and engagement quickly with their teams. Power structures are shifting and new approaches are evolving.

So, in this new context, leaders need to manage much change including transitional business risks as well as their own effectiveness. Coaching is one of the organizational responses to these changed circumstances and while the coaching industry is still evolving and maturing, coaches and companies offering coaching services are likely to be required to clarify and contract around desired visible change and demonstratable results. These results can range from behavioural change to other more commercial related results.

This book offers an evidence-based framework for understanding Leadership Transition Coaching. The framework is based on a research study undertaken in 2017 that explored the nuances of the leader's individual experience with leaders coming from both the private and public sectors. Five males and three females were interviewed using semi-structured interviews and a qualitative analysis was undertaken.

Four themes were generated and a clear picture of the impact of coaching emerged. They are *Time to Think, Clarity and Focus, Collaboration with Others* and *Development*. These four themes provide an overview of the key aspects that were important to the leaders as they transitioned to a new role. Subordinate themes were generated for each of the four main themes and will be outlined in each of the relevant chapters dedicated to the four themes. Leaders exhibited individual differences and an emphasis on different aspects of coaching, illustrating that there is no one size that fits all.

However, there was a definite consensus on specific aspects of the impact of coaching, which will be discussed in the following chapters.

Further interviews with leaders in transition were carried out in 2020 and their experiences are reflected in case studies in Chapter 12.

2 Coaching leaders in transition

How important is the arrival of a new leader in a company whether it is their first leadership role or they have held a number of leadership roles or have arrived at the CEO position or chairperson of the board? While responsibility escalates with the seniority of the role, leadership transitions are personal and their arrival creates expectations, both their own and others.

While context is important in terms of the size of their remit and influence, every leader taking on a new role is embarking at a unique time and will need to get to grips with the systems and dynamics of the new environment, so how can they be supported to best navigate and ultimately deliver their vision and strategy?

Leadership changes are more common than ever before. According to Keller and Meaney (2018), in a McKinsey report 69 per cent of new CEOs reshuffle their management teams within the first two years; transitions then cascade through the senior ranks. In total, 67 per cent of leaders report that their organizations now experience 'some or many more' transitions than they did in the previous year.

With the level of potential derailment estimated at 50 per cent for leaders within the first 18 months, coaching can support leaders with transition, which can reduce the potential risk. Hogan, Hogan and Kaiser (2011) provide a summary of results from 12 published estimates of the base rate of managerial failure, which range from 30 to 67 per cent, with an average of about 50 per cent.

They go on to provide previous research from Bentz (1985) who pioneered the study of managerial derailment. In a 30-year study of failed managers at Sears Roebuck and Company, Bentz (1985, as cited in Hogan, Hogan and Kaiser 2011: 5) noted that all the managers were intelligent, with social skills. They failed:

> because they: (1) lacked business skills, (2) were unable to deal with complexity, (3) were reactive and tactical, (4) were unable to delegate, (5) were unable to build a team, (6) were unable to maintain relationships with a network of contacts; (7) let emotions cloud their judgement, (8) were slow to learn, and (9) had an 'overriding personality defect'.

McCall and Lombardo (1983: 11) noted that the causes of derailment are 'all connected to the fact that situations change as one ascends the organizational hierarchy'. Others have also observed that most derailment occurs after a transition to a more senior role (such as Gentry and Chappelow 2009; Kovach

1989; Watkins 2003). Promotion brings more responsibility and scrutiny, more ambiguous performance expectations, and more complex politics according to Zaccaro (2001).

Further, senior jobs require a strategic perspective and the ability to build coalitions, negotiate, delegate, empower and use more participative decision-making to accomplish goals according to Charan, Drotter and Noel (2001). Kaiser and Craig (2011) in their study indicate that length of time in a leadership role is not a guarantee of success as the leader moves into a new role at a different level. Sejeli and Mansor (2015) believe that most cases of leadership derailment are predictable and can even be overcome.

Furthermore, statistics on failure rates and causes were taken from a number of landmark studies that were compiled by McKinsey Management Consultancy (Keller and Meaney 2018). Findings from those studies show that two years after leadership transitions, anywhere between 27 and 46 per cent of them are regarded as failures or disappointments. In this study, leaders ranked politics as the main challenge: 68 per cent of transitions founder on issues related to politics, culture and people, and 67 per cent wish they had moved faster to change the culture. In total, 79 per cent of external and 69 per cent of internal hires report that implementing culture change is difficult. Bear in mind that these are senior leaders who demonstrated success and showed intelligence, initiative and results in their previous roles.

An HR Outlook survey in the CIPD Winter 2015/2016 report (CIPD 2016) asked 143 HR leaders and 152 non-HR leaders to examine topics, trends and challenges affecting the HR profession. In this report, leadership capability was identified as one of the top challenges that 'keeps them awake at night'.

There were positive views regarding their technical skills of leaders but views were less positive around the leadership and people management skills. All the more reason why organizations need to provide support for leaders so that they have the competence and confidence to manage both the technical and people management aspects of their role, particularly in areas such as employee engagement, team development, managing change along with their own and their team's resilience and well-being.

Organizations can too readily treat new leadership transitions as a one-off event where new leaders are left to self-manage their transitions. Other organizations put supports in place such as linking the new leader with a peer or business buddy, assigning a mentor or coach to them or arranging for the leader to attend a specific learning and development programme.

Some methods, for instance tailored executive coaching and customized assimilation plans, have been shown to double the likelihood of success, but only 32 per cent of organizations use assimilation plans (Wheeler 2008).

In response to some of the needs for specific leadership support, the research undertaken by the authors sought to find out what the key aspects are of the impact of coaching on leaders as they navigate in real-time the changes and issues they encounter when making the move into a new role.

In an organizational setting, when new leaders take up their new role, their arrival creates expectations and impacts the dynamics within the organization. Below are a number of areas that highlight the impact of such change.

Newcomers to senior leadership

Making that move to a new leadership role can be both exciting and tinged with a hint of underlying anxiety relating to new uncertainties. It is a significant step change moving into a new senior leadership role even when a leader has made transitions in the past. Length of service or age are not protectors against potential anxieties that can arise in an unfamiliar territory.

As humans, we are hardwired for safety and significant change can impact the sympathetic nervous system of the most experienced leaders. While vulnerability and signs of doubt or stress may not be shown outwardly, they can be carried inwardly by the leader. Even previously resilient new leaders can find that they are tested when they step into more senior roles.

That step up can mean less contact with their teams and peers and known territory. Their confidence can take a dip for a while and they may need to consider their own further development as they take on the role while also considering the developmental stage of the team they will be leading.

Coaching can be viewed as a supportive process to ease the transition and to make the journey less stressful. According to Smith's (2015) research results, leaders reported that coaching helped with resilience in a number of ways. It helped them reclaim their self-belief, it contributed to their learning, it helped them see the wider perspective, it provided a supportive relationship and gave them a thinking space

Leadership resilience

Resilience can be defined as having that inner resource that is the capacity to rebound or bounce back from adversity, conflict, failure or even more positive events such as promotion and progress, which can carry with them increased responsibility. Luthans (2002) proposes that resilience is one of four essential psychological capabilities (PsyCap) for any successful leader, in addition to hope, optimism and confidence.

It is nearly a given with twenty-first-century leadership that the accelerated pace and context of organizational life calls for quick adaptation and significant resilience. Both of these are areas that coaching can support leaders in addressing. According to Smith (2015), while the development of certain cognitive strategies is helpful, participants also expressed the importance of the supportive coaching relationship when they encountered challenges or roadblocks and where resilience was required.

Leaders may talk about emotional and physical symptoms when their resilience is reduced. Their capacity to think rationally takes a hit, and they can easily find themselves triggered into fight, flight or freeze so their reactions are felt in the body as much as the mind. Different people are triggered in different ways, depending on personality and life experience.

An individual with a tendency to perfectionism, or someone with a deep need to control, is triggered differently from the person whose inclinations are to avoid conflict and who needs to feel liked. A recovery strategy that works for one person won't necessarily work for someone else. Some people surprise themselves with their ability to recover from setbacks, while for others it is much harder.

It is also worth noting that triggers are encounters or events that can catch a person and almost knock the person off balance with an emotional or physical response when they were feeling just fine before. If resilience is already low, a person may be more vulnerable to a trigger than they would otherwise have been. Leaders can be quite aware of what could trigger them.

For instance, a leader can report feeling overwhelmed by a crisis, whether at work or in personal life or everyday life, at work and at home. They may feel stuck with a situation or problem and unable to see the way forward. They may be trapped by perfectionism in themselves or others, compromised in their personal values, distressed by someone else's behaviours or frustrated by the organization.

So, the very act of a leader talking about their triggers can help them reflect and understand their own thought processes and behaviours around what makes them vulnerable to certain stimuli. They start to reflect on where these thoughts and behaviours are coming from and can possibly trace them back to earlier experiences. Knowing themselves better is a key ingredient to strengthening resilience.

A step for the coach can be to explore with the leader why they are doing what they are doing, regardless of the pressures. So, in the bigger scheme of things, considering their purpose and what motivates and what they really care about can ground and help to anchor the leader. A supportive and trusting relationship such as coaching can call out thoughts, emotions, beliefs and assumptions that need to be discussed with the aim of moving the leader on.

Emotions are contagious and leaders influence so much of the positive energy and emotion that needs to be developed in their teams. Psychological safety is an important component for a leader to be aware of if they have goals around their own and others' resilience, well-being and performance levels.

Q 1 – What motivates you?
Q 2 – What drains your energy?
Q 3 – What brings your energy?
Q 4 – What are some recent helpful insights about yourself?

Insight from neuroscience

While I am not advocating that an understanding of neuroscience is essential for coaches, I do think it brings insights from studies in this field, which can be helpful for both coaches and the leaders they coach. Brann (2014) highlights the importance of being able to supress irrelevant information such as distractions. This is important in order to prevent overloading limited working memory capacity.

In simple terms, our ability to remember relevant information depends on our ability to limit interference from irrelevant information. Constant interruptions on your smartphone and devices are deadly for prolonged focus and hamper getting the most out of your working memory. And, of course, stress impairs working memory, too, so if your client is stressed they can't expect to have their working memory in optimal working condition.

So where focus and even overload is a challenge for the leader, it will be useful to explore what may be getting their attention during their daily routines. All the more important that the leader can find thinking space such as that which coaching provides and where the leader can get access to the clarity and focus they need to navigate the new territory.

Separately, in earlier work through a series of books on the *Inner Game*, Tim Gallwey (2001) studied how internal interferences impacted performance and explained it in a simple equation:

$$P = p - i$$
$$(\text{Performance} = \text{potential} - \text{interferences})$$

Interferences can also be created internally through self-doubt, anxieties or negative self-talk.

Managing interferences can help maintain focus and energy. Even building in moments of mindfulness can create habits that reduce interference. Becoming aware of external and internal interferences can be a small step that can have big impact.

Some questions to reflect on:

- How important is this awareness in terms of the habits we are often unconsciously aware of in this 24/7 switched-on world we live in?
- Have you screened your thoughts today?
- What is the impact to well-being?
- What are your communication preferences, email, call, online platforms, face-to-face, and expectations around availability and working across time zones with your team?
- How far down do you intend to push the decision-making process?
- Could this insight be something to consider in terms of building resilience for both you and your team?

Leveraging strengths

As the coach considers ways to support the leader in developmental ways to enhance resilience, the coach may consider this a good time to explore what the leader sees as their strengths. A strengths assessment can be a good intervention here and is useful when working in the area of resilience. It can help the leader to calibrate their strengths in so far as understanding more about strengths and explore what can happen if strengths are overplayed. Gentry and Chappelow (2009) found research to show that derailment could result from strengths or from the overuse of a personality strength that becomes a defence and could also become a derailer.

At the same time, leaders can often discount something they are good at because they simply don't recognize it in themselves, taking it for granted. On the other hand, they take a strength too far by thinking that this is what got them where they are today, failing to recognize the signals that the environment has changed and so need they.

Leaders need to be keenly attuned to sensing situations, knowing what is the right thing to do and when to do it. 'Versatile leadership' is the phrase used by Kaplan and Kaiser (2006) to convey this, making the case that we all tend to veer to one or other pole of any leadership dichotomy – with 'forceful-enabling' and 'strategic-operational' being the people and process parameters on which Kaplan and Kaiser focus. Versatile leaders who can do both seamlessly perform much better than those who cannot: as the data show, leadership versatility predicts as much as 42 per cent of the variance in overall leadership effectiveness (Kaiser, Lindberg and Craig 2007).

As a development tool, I can recommend *The Top 5 Clifton Strengths* report, which can be sourced via the Gallup organization on www.strengthsfinder .com. The client can undertake the online assessment and download the report, which is focused on their top five strengths, which can be a valuable resource for a client. As the coach works with a client, they can consider how they can use their strengths in the role and also consider if any of these strengths are overplayed, what the impact may be.

Behavioural change – diving below the surface

Coaching can have a significant calming, balancing and responsibility-enhancing effect on personality, and executive coaching can be very relevant at top levels of organizational leadership. A supportive and trusting relationship can evoke thoughts, emotions, beliefs and assumptions that need to be discussed, with the aim of moving the leader forward. Coaching conversations allow for deep conversations, which can touch on the unconscious behaviours that can be explored in a safe environment. The leader can gain perspective through a wider lens through reflection on situations.

Jean Piaget, a Swiss psychologist and pioneer in the field of cognitive development, introduced the idea of 'schema'. A schema is the person's way of processing information and how they develop their thought and behavioural patterns which are shaped from early life experiences. This mental structure is built on preconceived ideas that become 'ways of knowing'. Schemas are organized knowledge structures through which we encode our perceptions of social interaction, allowing us to make sense of our own behaviour and the behaviour of others (Fong and Markus 1982; Kihlstrom and Klein 1994; Markus 1977; Sedikides 1993; Young, Klosko and Weishaar 2003).

According to Nelson and Hogan (2009), schemas function automatically outside of conscious awareness. They note where there is the probability of dysfunctional behaviour, this reflects the strength of the relevant underlying schema.

Separately, that may explain why one person is triggered by certain situational factors while another person is not affected in the same way. This scenario can leave the person's behaviour appearing irrational to someone else. When under stress and strain these automatic behavioural responses are more likely to appear, like sharpened tools ready to respond with efficiency.

These automatic short-cuts are embedded behaviour and exist for the most part at an unconscious level. Once schemas are formed, they have a tendency to remain unchanged and people build their understanding and ideas, which are like guides on auto-pilot helping the person navigate the world, never questioning if those ideas are still true and helpful.

So each leader and coach show up with their own schema (mental model) and will be working together with their own basic beliefs about themselves and the world around them. A leader in transition will be navigating and making sense of the new environment amidst all the other individual, team, groups, cultural and organizational dynamics. So at a time when the leader's mental processing will be stretched, the coaching relationship may be the only real relationship where the leader can reflect on situations, behavioural responses of self and others and gain understanding in a safe and respectful way. The transitioning leaders might find it easier to navigate their way forward when they use tools like reflective learning, taking action and reviewing what happened between sessions, which all help to build experience and possibly raise confidence levels.

Furthermore, coaching can have a significantly beneficial effect on a leader's potential personality derailers, especially where the leader overplays behaviours deriving from a kind of personality overdrive that can get the individual into trouble, regardless of their high achievements and results orientation.

Richard, a senior leader who participated in the research, spoke about his experience:

> I can find myself the odd time fighting battles I shouldn't be bothered about. So, I think ego is probably the biggest thing or pride or whatever it is. I gave up sport about three or four years ago and I became an awful lot more competitive at work as a result and I think that is kind of part of it.
>
> Maybe I don't have the patience to play the system. I can be seen as a bit brash and a bit arrogant sometimes. I am aware that I am but it just comes out of me [laugh] so it is the ego thing.
>
> I had been brought onto the senior leadership group in Company X and I think I may have been considered before, but I kind of reined in my brashness a bit and I think I wouldn't have got that opportunity if I had been as brash as I originally had been. So yeah, it probably wouldn't have happened but it was a result of it [the coaching].

Organizations can avail of assessment tools such as the Hogan assessment suite of reports either prior to or as part of the selection process. An assessment can also form part of a learning and development initiative in preparedness for progression or sometime after the leader's appointment. These reports are instruments that provide information on personality traits.

Such reports can be a useful guide for the leader to gain insight into their behavioural strengths but also consider, if some behaviours are underplayed or overplayed, what the implications might be. This can be particularly relevant when reflecting on the context of the new role and business environment along with the culture of the organization.

Other avenues to insight for the leader as they make the journey of transition into the new role include 360-degree feedback, employee feedback surveys, taking a look at employee turnover, absenteeism rates. Turnaround of information is also happening at a pace so quick adaptation is a pre-requisite in today's world.

A tool I have found useful for quick feedback is to ask:

What should I start doing, stop doing, continue doing?

A leader can give feedback to a team member using this question. Similarly the team member can be asked to give feedback that may be helpful for the leader, so the sharing of feedback is a two-way process. This is also a useful question for a leader or facilitator to use when working with a team. It is a focused intervention that can be frank, open and honest once it is undertaken with good intention.

Some personality traits can be difficult to deal with, where the person's behaviour may appear somewhat, volatile, arrogant or overtly domineering. Self-promoting, manipulative behaviour, with a lack of emotion or morality, can be described as a 'dark side' to personality. Some of these traits thrive in competitive environments. Also, these dysfunctional traits are likely to be more evident in times of stress.

Whether becoming a leader or having arrived at the most senior level, dark personality traits can play havoc in an organization creating a toxic environment that can impact team morale and engagement, along with impacting well-being. It is worth noting that skills development approaches will fail if the leader has low intrapersonal self-regulation or flawed interpersonal strategies.

This level of change is not always possible on a development programme due to the nature of the learning setting. Gurdjian, Halbeisen and Lane (2014) write that identifying some of the deepest 'below the surface' thoughts, feelings, assumptions and beliefs is usually a precondition of behavioural change – one too often shirked in development programmes. A psychologically safe work environment is greatly influenced by the leader and is even more important in times of crisis or high stress.

Helena one of the research participants spoke of her experience:

People do look to you, they do, when they get doubts in their head is when you really have to and when the going gets tough, that's when you really have to stay true to yourself.

In today's world, leaders navigating transition to any new role are faced with unprecedented levels of change. In 2020, the COVID-19 pandemic has had far-reaching affects across the globe and similar to the 'butterfly effect', something that initially appears as small can have a big impact. Leaders today need to be prepared and supported more than ever as they, with their teams and stakeholders, collaborate to achieve organizational outcomes that also have an impact on society and the wider environment.

Leaders and their organizations now have to make tough decisions on how they plan to sustain the business when there is still a lot of uncertainty. They need to stay open to what they don't know and see the value in collaborating with others to take in different perspectives. The whole is greater than the sum of its parts is a phrase that comes to mind and in today's world there is an emerging understanding that the leader does not have magical powers but can work side by side and influence the dynamics, performance and innovation that is inherent within the team.

Building relationships and trust is important and as Helena, one of the senior leaders in the research indicated, this is something that can be so easily taken for granted but if that trust gets broken, then it becomes so much harder to build up again.

> So, I suppose I put a huge emphasis on relationships. I always would have had but I think the value of them and how easy they are to damage and how precious they are and how hard they are to build back up.

Coaching can support individuals in better regulating and directing their intra-personal and interpersonal resources through self-directed learning. While coaches can find themselves in uncomfortable places at times, this is where their own maturity and development comes into play. How they can hold themselves in uncomfortable places and continue to do good work but also knowing when to refer out to other sources is important. The world of coaching can at times come close to what might be determined as psychotherapy, so the coach always needs to be mindful of when they could be starting to stray into the therapeutic zone.

The characteristics of the coach in terms of their own training, experience, style and practice is unique and fundamental to the coaching experience. Such scenarios endorse more than ever the value of coaching supervision where a coach can find that space to reflect and replenish their own energy and resources, and develop within their own coaching practice.

Thinking styles

Thinking styles are specific reasoning and problem-solving strategies that help people respond to different problems that need to be solved in their work or personal lives. They are developed from the experiences and meaning making part of our cognition. They are influenced by our attitudes, interest and feelings about a given task or situation. It is worth doing an online search on *unhelpful thinking styles*, which can be useful for both coaches and their clients to reflect on.

In an exploratory study carried out in 2009 by Murphy and Janeke on the relationship between thinking styles and emotional intelligence, the results show that thinking styles are significant predictors of emotional intelligence and that participants who have high emotional intelligence prefer more complex and creative thinking styles.

Mindset

In essence, people create their own realities and how they see things is directly related to what they have experienced, what they have read, who they have met and where they have lived. People create core beliefs and run their own stories and narratives, which run automatically and often without ever having been questioned.

As mentioned earlier, when beliefs are challenged people can have a response similar to the feeling of being physically attacked and they can counteract the feeling by fighting even more for the belief. So, beliefs are strong and are part of the meaning-making machine that helps people survive. For the most part, beliefs can serve people well alongside the fact that people have been known to die for their beliefs.

And that is just to highlight the power of beliefs. Leaders in transition will bring with them beliefs that have supported them in the past and while some beliefs will still serve them well, others may impede their way forward.

It's true that some personality traits (such as extraversion or introversion) are ways of being, but people can change the way they see the world and their values. Gurdjian, Halbeisen and Lane (2014) looked at a professional-services business that wanted senior leaders to initiate more provocative and meaningful discussions with the firm's senior clients. Once the trainers on the development programme looked below the surface, they discovered that these leaders, though highly successful in their fields, were instinctively uncomfortable and lacking in confidence when conversations moved beyond their narrow functional expertise. As soon as the leaders realized this, and went deeper to understand why, they were able to commit themselves to concrete steps that helped push them to change.

What happens where the leader may need to respond to the new context, which may present challenges that they were not expecting? For example, leaders moving from a large company to a start-up need to recognize that expectations are likely to be different in the new setting. They may have to consciously adjust their style to embrace the informality of the new work environment and the level of procedure and supports they previously encountered may not be readily available to them.

Likewise, moving from a smaller company with a short history, which may have a more informal approach, is significantly different to a large organization with a longer history behind it and with established procedures and possible multiple cultures across the business. So a shift in mindset is likely required to 'get their head' around the new context. As much as the leader considers their own mindset, they will also start to get insights to mindsets of the team they will lead.

Inner resources for sustaining well-being and performance

There are a number of thought leaders whose research has focused on how people can build their inner resources such as mindset and set themselves up for success. These ideas are not 'aspirational' but rather they are drawn from rigorous research carried out by Carol Dweck, American psychologist at Stanford University, Dr Maureen Gaffney, Irish clinical psychologist and Dr Martin Seligman, American psychologist, all who provide insights that challenge old world views that can be self-limiting. It is worth taking a brief look at the topics of mindset, emotions and positive psychology.

Carol Dweck is a Stanford psychologist and author of *Mindset: The New Psychology of Success* (2016). In her research she found two distinct mindsets. One is a *fixed mindset* where the person believes their personal qualities and characteristics are static or carved in stone and their response to failure is perceived as fatal. According to Carol Dweck, it's the power of the little word 'yet' that can make all the difference.

In a world depleted of hope; in a world of wanting what we want, when we want; it expresses our required patience and belief in one's self or another person's abilities to realize that some things are worth waiting for and those things take work and sometimes they don't always come in.

Another person with a *growth mindset* perceives that their personal qualities and characteristics can be somewhat adapted through effort while also taking the view that if they fail at something they can learn from the situation. So a person's relationship with success and failure are important considerations – just think how the mindset of a leader can impact psychological safety, creativity and innovation within an organization.

What is the impact of an overly competitive mindset? Which mindset is likely to lean towards developing collaborative relationships? Which mindset is likely to develop talent within the organization? Does the leader see value in considering the psychological dimensions of their work as a leader? Coaches equally can bring their own experience and insights to discussions with their client.

Carol Dweck's *Two Mindsets* is worth doing a search on to gain insight into the elements of these two different mindsets.

All the more reason that mindfulness has become such a powerful medium for managing thoughts and building awareness, which is beneficial to well-being, ultimately sustaining performance. So, for leaders, who influence so much, it is important for them to consider the beliefs and values they bring to their leadership role. Are they likely to encourage and promote growth mindsets within the team they will lead?

Psychologist Maureen Gaffney, author of the book *Flourishing* (2011) looked at the impact of emotions on people's lives. Evidence from her research shows that for every one negative emotion a person has, which can drag them down, it will take three positive emotions to lift them up again.

In order to really flourish, it will take five positive emotions for every one negative emotion a person is experiencing. In other words, to offset the effect of every burst of irritability, every tense exchange, every negative thought and feeling of disappointment it requires, not double, but five times as many positives to stay in a state of flourishing. The research goes on to show that, on average, people are living their lives in a ratio of 2:1 and are, in effect, languishing.

So even to consider reaching three positive emotions to every one negative emotion keeps life in a steady state. If a person processes on average 70,000 thoughts a day, it is worth considering the quality of those thoughts and how helpful they are as thoughts feed emotions. Emotions are also known to be contagious, so other people's emotions can have impact on people around them.

A leader's emotions will be picked up quicker by team members over any of their peers. According to study undertaken by Sy, Côté and Saavedra (2005), they found that groups with leaders in a positive mood exhibited more coordination and expended less effort than did groups with leaders in a negative mood. While leaders in transition are focused on delivering results, their personal energy and resilience needs to be sustained.

With this in mind, it is useful to look to the field of positive psychology and the work of Martin Seligman who became the president of the APA (American Psychological Association) in 1998. At this juncture in his career, he set about changing the narrow view of traditional psychology, which looked at what depleted people, and he started to focus on what helped people flourish.

From here, he carried out research to understand other factors in human nature such as resilience. His first paper in the field of positive psychology was published in 2000 along with Mihaly Csikszentmihalyi who is the founder of the concept of 'flow'. One of the great benefits of PP (Positive Psychology) is that it teaches the power of shifting perspective. Martin Seligman in his 2012 book *Flourish: A Visionary New Understanding of Happiness and Well-being* describes a model he devised, known as PERMA (Positive Emotions, Engagement, Relationships, Meaning and Achievement). This model generates questions that can be reflected on:

P = What activities give you pleasure in life?
E = During which activities do you find yourself loosing track of time?
R = What relationships energize you and support you?
M = To what extent do you do things that you feel are valuable and worth-
       while to you?
A = Have you a goal you are working towards?

Leaders will be no strangers to challenge and opportunities. The challenges and opportunities of today's world can be complex and dynamic and a leader's mindset will be a resource that can hinder or help both themselves and the people they will lead and collaborate with.

In Victor Frankl's book, *Man's Search for Meaning* (1946/2008), his lived experience shows that everything can be taken away from a person except their ability to choose their attitude in any given set of circumstances. A person can frame their choices in ways that help them to make the best decision they can in an uncertain world. These insights are worth noting in terms of adaptive ways of being and are conducive not alone to building resilience but also to supporting a person's general well-being.

Again, I come back to the analogy whether as coach or leader, if professional helpers look after their own safety first by putting their own safety equipment on, they are in a better position to support others.

Emotional intelligence

Emotional intelligence (EQ) is one's ability to recognize and understand emotions in self and others and the ability to use this awareness to manage behaviour and relationships. Self-awareness is the foundation of emotional intelligence. Self-awareness requires understanding your emotions and how you react to various people and situations.

John, one of the research participants, shared his experience.

> I found the emotional intelligence very useful. That's where I was first introduced to emotional intelligence. It was during those coaching sessions and I persisted with it right through and that was in terms of . . . I suppose, I liked the idea of what I could do to improve myself. There weren't all these kinds of things that are fixed, like that you can't change.
>
> So that was why I liked the idea of coaching as a way to help me improve, to help me get better and I suppose it gave me that inner confidence that I could get better and if I applied myself and I suppose the process was about checking in with regarding what I learned and what I had applied.

According to Neale, Spencer-Arnell and Wilson (2011), areas of emotional intelligence can be changed but not through some 'quick fix' as evidence shows it takes 21 days to change an attitude or a habit.

Both as a coachee and coach, I have experience of working with the EQ-i2.0 and EQ360 reports, which measure emotional intelligence. These assessments can provide rich personal feedback for leaders.

Cognitive behavioural coaching (CBC)

Cognitive behavioural coaching (CBC) derives from the work of two leading cognitive behavioural theorists, researchers and therapists, Aaron Beck (1976) and Albert Ellis (1962) whose original work in this field collectively comes under the convention of cognitive behavioural therapy (CBT).

What CBC offers to coaches is an in-depth understanding of how self-defeating beliefs are developed and then maintained in the face of contradictory evidence (e.g. despite an excellent work record, a client believes they are not good enough for a senior position because they continually discredit their achievements).

What often blocks the way are the client's self-limiting/defeating thoughts and beliefs (e.g. 'I can't afford to make any mistakes'), counterproductive behaviours (e.g. indecisiveness) and troublesome emotions (e.g. prolonged anxiety). Public speaking or speaking in front of groups of people is a skill that most leaders need to carry out with ease. Yet public speaking can be very uncomfortable for some people and they may even take on coaching specifically with that goal in mind.

CBC helps clients to identify, examine and change such thoughts and beliefs, develop productive behaviours and become more skilled at emotional management.

ABCDE model (Neenan and Dryden, 2000, 2002) is a framework used in CBC:

A = Activating event or other people
Identify the event that causes stress or triggers a threat – Activating event or other people
B = Belief (self-limiting or defeating belief)
Examine the logic around the belief system and why it has developed
C = Consequences (emotional intensity, physical, behavioural)
Explore the emotional and psychological consequences of this belief
D = Disputing or examining the limiting or self-defeating beliefs
Does this belief still make sense or is it even part of another underlying belief?
E = Effective outlook that is a new way of looking at the event
Deconstructing and releasing the unhelpful belief and taking on a new belief

Note in the ABCDE model, the coach needs to emphasize that A (events or other people) does not cause C (but contributes to it); B (beliefs) largely determines C (consequences). This is an empowering view of how change occurs because it allows the person to develop different beliefs (moving from D to E) about A (the initial event or person), which consequently modify the client's reactions at C.

It is useful to note that if A really did cause C, it would be very difficult, if not impossible, to change at C and would mean that the clients' emotional destiny would be at the mercy of events or lie in the hands of others.

When a client appears to feel stuck around an issue to do with an event or other people, the ABCDE model can be a useful coaching approach. It does not offer a quick fix, so the new patterns of thinking need to be tried out and tested over time, until confidence is gained and the new thought patterns are embedded.

The coach while using CBC is monitoring to identify any beliefs either clearly visible or very subtle that are having an adverse impact on the leader's progress and this also includes the coach's own beliefs such as, 'I've got to keep asking questions to impress my client and not let any silences occur as this indicates incompetence', which results in the coach's preoccupation with his/her next question instead of listening to the client and squeezing out of the session any reflective space. This level of attention will form the coach's own awareness of their own processing and may be a topic for consideration when the coach attends their own coach supervision.

A key question that can be asked by coaches is: 'Where is the cut-off point between coaching and counselling?' This question usually refers to a client in coaching who is showing a degree of psychological distress and how long should the coach persevere in trying to deal with it? This depends on the coach's skills, background and experience.

A guide for referral might be the intensity, frequency and duration of psychological distress and its impact on the coaching process, e.g. is the client able to focus on the goal-directed issues in the sessions and successfully carry out the agreed actions between them? There will be times when a coach will meet a leader dealing with psychological difficulties and it is therefore necessary for the coach to know his or her limitations and cut-off point. So, if in doubt, refer it out (to other professional services that will be able to assist the client).

Gestalt coaching

A gestalt psychological view is that what we see and how we perceive things is not an objective reality but the result of who we are at one moment in time. What makes sense in a particular context changes momentarily. In an attempt to organize the dynamic complexity of experience, people tend to arrange things in a way that makes sense according to their current thinking, prior experience or preoccupations.

People are also predisposed to look for symmetry and equilibrium or 'closure'. Experiments with our visual process give us some understanding of the way our perception of the world is self-directed. You may have seen the image that depicts a face and/or candle stick (depending on how you perceive it). It is a good example of how people's visual perceptions come into play. It is also a mindful reminder how people can see and experience the same thing so differently.

People also have a tendency to favour similarity, seeing patterns, grouping similar items together and differentiating them from others.

Leaders reinterpret their world in some way in the light of new experiences and thus their understanding of who they are through their experiences is continually shifting. An aim of gestalt coaching is to explore this subjective world in a way that enables the leader to access a wider range of choices and make the most of their capacities.

The relationship between coach and coachee is real and equal, with the coach facilitating a deepening process of awareness, and the coachee as a result becoming more whole and capable of finishing unfinished business. The accent is on the here-and-now and experiencing what is in the moment, including the relationship between coach and coachee. In a gestalt coaching setting, the leader may expect the coach to pay detailed attention to the client's feelings, physical movements and body language, watch the client's breathing, tone of voice, language and all that actually occurs within the session and the coach enquires into them or reflects them back. If coaches sense that something is being held back, they can enquire about that too. The coach may find their intuition is helpful in the process as much as logical thought.

According to Allan and Whybrow (2008: 136), 'gestalt coaching is lively and alive because the coach will always be seeking to uncover what has to be changed right here and now in this room so that change can happen effectively outside it and at another time'.

Gestalt coaching facilitates awareness through encouraging the client to enter into a conversation with the critical or 'other', split-off part of themselves. Gestalt coaching is present-oriented, but the dialogue may provide a way of drawing out beliefs, assumptions and values that have been learned through earlier experiences, illustrating patterns of perception.

The client can then examine thoughts, feelings and behaviour and can then make a conscious choice what to retain and what to let go. A number of techniques such as the 'two chair' exercise, 'meta-mirror' and visualization are examples of gestalt work.

Awareness comes from being in the moment with the client in what is a very safe space. The coach is not there to find a solution for the client nor to fall into confluence with the client. The coach is there as a keen observer allowing clients to find their own truth through accessing a deeper awareness of themselves.

Confidence can dip in unknown territory

According to Evers, Brouwers and Tomic (2006), coaching has become a valuable support, particularly in times of transition. They carried out quasi experiments in a controlled and experimental group and findings from their empirical results indicate that coaching was effective with regards to improving self-efficacy beliefs. Leaders need to have belief in their own capability while they also need to build trust and belief in others, with whom they will collaborate to deliver results.

Equally, a coach can experience self-doubt and an unknowing at moments in the coaching conversation. De Haan (2008: 105) noted 'the effectiveness of coaches seems determined primarily by their ability to doubt, not to know what is coming next, and to greet what comes next with questions'.

All of the leaders in the research referred to the importance of trust that is built up with their coach. This trust creates the psychological safety that enables the leader to openly share and express doubts or uncomfortable thoughts that may not otherwise get aired. Ultimately, if those thoughts are shaky, they can undermine the leader's confidence.

Equally, the coach can explore and challenge the leader on those thoughts. Also, leaders as they move to more senior roles, and particularly when they move to another organization, can have that felt sense of being alone as they navigate the journey of their own change.

Trust needs to be built up with the coach and if it is not developed, the leader's ability to be fully present and open with the coach is compromised. This space of trust is mutually created between the coach and the leader. Over time, this trust creates the psychological safety that allows the leader to openly share thoughts and any doubts that might otherwise never get aired.

For leaders to have opportunities to share openly in a safe space in organizations is rare enough and less so for leaders in a world that is communicating 24/7 and where communication is open to interpretation through multiple forms of media.

The coach can be that safe sounding board for the leader as they talk through what is on their mind. Emotions, much more than facts and trends, shape our realities. The more uncertain the leader is about something, the more he/she can imagine it and believe it exists. The leader may have experienced an encounter that has left them feeling unsettled and this can lead to theories being created without clear evidence.

Instead of rationally discussing these fears with the leader, a useful technique for the coach is to play back what they hear the leader say and the emotions they are noticing. This can be the opening for the leader to examine their story and to contemplate facts from fear. The coach may also be curious to know if there is anything else that is coming into awareness and this can be a time where beliefs and assumptions become clearer and can now be considered in a new light.

In times of crisis or uncertainty, the leader more than ever needs to hear the narrative of their own story before they can embody change in their thoughts and feelings. This can also have the effect of helping the leader build resilience by staying energized and resourceful. This can also be an opportunity for the coach to enquire what the leader now wants instead of what is occurring.

While a leader may still be unclear as to the desired state, at least the question can become the doorway to the beginning of a way forward. In the early days of my introductory training to business coaching with Sean Weafer, author of *The Business Coaching Revolution* (2001), I was introduced to two concepts that have stayed with me over the years and they are the:

- G2S model (global to specific), which refers to breaking down of a global goal or challenge. The concept of the word 'global' here is the perceived goal or challenge in its entirety. By breaking down the perceived goal or challenge to more detailed specifics or smaller elements, the client can gain more clarity and a wider perspective, where they can now consider options and create solutions that achieve the greater goal or challenge. And in the authors' recent research, some of the leaders referred to the value of being able to do a 'download' and the clarity that comes from that.
- CIA model that through a series of three questions helped the client consider potential options to the issue being discussed and can be helpful if a client feels stuck in the issue.

1 Can I **control** the situation (Yes or No or Maybe)?
2 Can I **influence** the situation (Yes or No or Maybe)?
   If the answer is no to both of above then enquire
3 Can I **accept** this situation for now? All things change over time whether they be good, bad or indifferent.

To think that everything stays the same forever can be a self-limiting belief. So, shifting the mindset can create a new perspective on the situation being addressed.

Core strategic competency – making an effective leadership transition

As indicated earlier, the pace of change has significantly accelerated and new leaders are expected to show results soon after their arrival which leans on the credibility of the new leader to perform confidently. According to Levin (2010), how leaders and their organizations effectively manage such role transitions is likely to become a strategic capability, such as a core strategic competency, with clear bottom-line implications for their organization.

The first 100 days has become a marker when moving into new roles. So, considering the investment that has been made to bring the new leader thus far and to avoid risk, coaching new leaders can have a strategic impact in supporting the effective transition both for the new leader and the wider organization.

3 | Leaders' experience of the new territory

You may have heard the phrase from Alfred Korzybski 'the map is not the territory' (Pula 1996: 87) and this concept holds equally true for a transitioning leader, arriving into a new role. Expectations have been building on all sides with the arrival of the leader and the reality of these expectations can only be revealed over time.

When we expect to see things from only one point of view, it can be self-limiting. Anais Nin once cited the Talmudic saying 'We do not see the world as it is, but as we are' (1961). So, to work consciously and to take stock of our environment and our individual reactions, by becoming self-aware we can allow ourselves to see that there can be a broader context at play.

The context of moving into a new role is a totally new experience for the leader. The leader will be making meaning of their new world. The transitioning leaders will be calling on their perspective of their own way of knowing from previous experiences and assimilating that with new information that will be reaching them through their senses and intuition. So, it all combines to create a unique time for the leaders where they now have choice in terms of how they will be as a leader moving forward.

Will what brought them success in the past continue to bring them success in the future? Is the leader's way of knowing all encompassing and sufficient to cross the trajectory of the new role in its wider sense? What beliefs, habits and assumptions are embedded, that might now need to be reviewed and where do one's values fit in? So much of the invisible forces of leadership and organizational life can be about fitting into the culture, while a leader's role may be to transform the culture.

Coaching allows leaders time and a safe space to capitalize on their experience as they consider what they need to stop, start or continue doing as they navigate their way forward in the new role

Leader transitions – impact on wider organization

As leaders' transition to new roles they also need to consider the impact of their new role on the wider organization. As Bond and Naughton (2011: 167) in an article in *International Coaching Psychology Review* noted, 'a distinctive feature of leadership transitions is the impact on other parts of the organization, creating the need to manage the transitional business risks as well as the individual effectiveness risks'.

Expectations by the leader's manager, his or her direct reports and teams within the leader's business function, other stakeholders, both internally and externally, where business dependencies exist, all create a dynamic that calls on the visibility and effectiveness of the new leader. Additionally, the new leader's own expectations and perspectives are added to this context. The rapid pace of change, continuous technological development, global economies, with up to five generations in the workplace, all bring with it a new working dynamic that calls for adaptation at an accelerated rate.

With that can come the need for a paradigm shift to meet new opportunities and challenges that the leader may encounter. According to Manderscheid and Harrower (2016: 391) 'Leader transitions can be fraught with challenges as new leaders try to adapt to a new culture, team, and work processes'.

Transition is more than a change event

Much has been written on the topic of transition by Bridges and Mitchell (2000) who note that transition is not a change event. They view transition as the internal state: a psychological reorientation the leader will now have to go through before the change into the new can work successfully. The authors cite that most leaders imagine that transition is automatic – that it occurs simply because the change is happening. But it doesn't.

Bridges and Mitchell hold that transition takes longer because it requires that people undergo three separate processes and all of them can be upsetting. The first is that people say goodbye (endings) and let go of the way things used to be and personally for them it is the way that they themselves used to be. Leaders will need to leave where they are and what has brought them success in the past. This can feel like their world of experience, habits, their sense of identity and reality itself is being shaken.

On paper, the change looks like a logical shift, but the landscape has changed for the leader and in practice this means that his or her new role will call for new business relationships, new ways of working, new priorities, new levels of responsibility. Leaders' sense-making of their new world will take a paradigm shift. While staying with the first part of the transition process, it is important to consider whether the leader is moving within or outside the organization.

As noted by Ciampa (2016), it is important to recognize that the formal transfer of title and the new leader's arrival is not the end of the process. The new leader cannot be considered truly embedded until he or she wins the loyalty of the organization's most influential managers and that may not occur for months. It is signified not by an event but by behaviour.

Value of on-boarding the leader and avoiding derailment

Where an internal candidate has already navigated a career within the company, the on-boarding may seem unnecessary, but even an internal candidate will benefit from transition support that recognizes several specific challenges to be faced. Ciampa specifically referenced the transition for CEOs after the initial handshake: it is fair to say that leaders who are moving to more senior levels will need to navigate their unique transition journeys each time they move to a new role, whether this is a lateral or a horizontal move.

He noted that one-third to one-half of new chief executives fail within their first 18 months, according to some estimates. He states that some of the fall-outs can be attributed to poor strategic choices by the new leader and some result when the leader's skill-set does not fit the context. Poor hand-offs from the previous leader to new leader are also cited as a risk for the new incomer.

Ciampa (2016) notes three key mistakes such as (1) not reading the political situation well enough to build necessary relationships and coalitions; (2) not achieving the cultural changes the strategic and operational agendas require; (3) the incoming leaders overestimate the willingness or the capacity of the people they inherit to abandon old habits and behaviours.

Ciampa furthermore observes that existing senior key executives within the organization can add to the failure by (1) not understanding that hand-offs at the more senior levels are not as simple as at the lower levels; (2) failing to carefully consider the cultural and political aspects of the company that may be problematic for the new leader in the first few months; (3) setting one-dimensional or generic expectations for the new leaders, e.g. emphasizing financial and operational goals and not including equally specific cultural, political and personal ones.

The purpose of a comprehensive approach to transitioning is to avoid those mistakes. The transition establishes a solid path toward productive relationships between the new leader and key stakeholders.

The unknown unknown

The second phase of the transition according to Bridges and Mitchell (2000) is called the neutral zone and is that in-between state of getting to know the unknown, which brings some confusion and uncertainty and simply dealing with these aspects of the new landscape can take up a lot of people's energy. The neutral zone is where the explorations take place and this can feel uncomfortable, so people generally are driven to get out of it. Successful transition, however, requires that people spend some time in the neutral zone.

This time in the neutral zone is not wasted, for that is where the creativity and energy of transition are found and the real transformation takes place. This can be the stage where coaching is called upon to support the leader in navigating the journey to the new state. This will include both tangible resources such as taking time to think and plan a way forward, while also releasing the more intangible inner resources and strengths that the leader can tap into.

Disruption such as the world experienced with the health and economic challenges experienced with COVID-19 in 2020 presents leaders with unprecedented pressures.

Moving forward – new beginnings

The third part of the transition process is called 'moving forward' (new beginnings). This phase requires people to begin behaving in a new way. For leaders moving into a new role where they have to build new relationships reasonably quickly and hit the ground running and build in some quick wins, this can be disconcerting and it can put their sense of competence and value at risk.

Most leaders come from backgrounds where technical, financial, or operational skills were paramount, and those skills provide little help when it comes to leading people. Such leaders may be pushing the limits of their understanding of the future, and they need perspective and advice. That is where a trusted colleague, confidant, coach or consultant can offer valuable counsel to the leader.

This person's background or professional affiliation can vary widely; what matters is that she or he understands how to help people through transition. It is a role that is far more interpersonal and collaborative than is played by most consultants or trainers accustomed to teaching a skill or prescribing a solution.

4 Navigating the journey

Coaching the leader through the transition process

Leaders are in a better position to lead their team through future change when they understand and acknowledge the experience of the transition process themselves, even if that is seeking individualized assistance such as coaching.

This is a space where the new leader can *off-load* all that is pressing on their mind in a confidential and psychologically safe environment with her coach.

Through questions from the coach, the new leader can *get clarity* by putting everything on the table and start to *understand the key issues* to be addressed, *explore options*, *consider challenges and opportunities* and *plan a way forward*.

The discipline of working with a coach ensures the new leaders *facilitate time away* from the operations of the business to *create the future* they want to build and the coaching meetings are also a check-in point to *review* the actions discussed at the coaching sessions.

The coaching space allows the new leader time to *pause, reflect and learn* from situations that have shown up between the coaching meetings. So *reflective learning* and *learning in action* are ways of bringing about a sustainable shift that can also be seen in some of the *mindset shift* and *behavioural change* that can take place during the coaching process.

In a world of work that is accelerating with pace and space and with a global presence, coaching brings a unique time to think that allows the leaders to *show up at their best* where they can *succeed* both for themselves and the wider organization.

Bridges and Mitchell (2000) add that a good coach can help the leaders to discover their own *best approaches* and work with their own *goals, limitations* and *concerns* to create a *development plan* that prepares them for the future.

Times of transition are becoming the rule rather than the exception. Yet few leaders know how to prepare for the changes that lie ahead. Transition leadership skills must be congruent with and must *capitalize and build on the leader's own strengths and talents*. They cannot be found in a set of theoretical leadership skills.

The transition adviser (coach in this instance) works collaboratively with each leader to assess the leader's place in the three-part transition process, the *strengths the leader brings* and how to *leverage* them, and *what the current situation demands*. It is a *personal* and completely *customized* process.

Bridges (2004) notes that the extremely high level of change in today's organizations is likely to keep careers in a semi-permanent state of transition, due to re-organizations, mergers, technological changes, strategic shifts and a steady stream of new products and most organizations are in a constant stage of turmoil.

Systemic organizations

The uniqueness of people, organizations and environmental situations and context is a fact of life. A system is a series of interconnected, interdependent relationships and systems also have subsystems. The first system, culture, can be an example whereby a leader who moves to a new role in another organization or sometimes within the current organization can experience different approaches and different ways of doing things even though they work in the same professional field or industry. So, it can be limiting to assume that certain practices will work the same in a uniquely different environment.

Complexity and dynamics play a key role in the systemic view of organizations with the interplay of what happens both inside and outside the organization. Within the system, people are actors who have different personalities and also come with their own unique needs, fears, traits, capabilities, limitations and memories.

People's lives have both private and public aspects to them as they live their lives in different places such as communities and geographies and these, in turn, will influence them. People have to deal with various demands and aspects of their lives whether they be in their home lives or work lives or wherever they spend their time. Dealing with their time and resources to achieve outcomes will also be a factor. So, there are many different aspects at play

The first systems people belong to are their family system, education and cultural system. We instinctively know how we belong in these systems and learn what we need to do to protect ourselves in these systems that brings about a sense of belonging.

To deal with complexity, people build themselves patterns of action, behaviour and thinking that they can repeat, such as habits, rituals, rote behaviour, expectations, prejudices, sense constructs and views of the world. These patterns reduce complexity to a more acceptable, manageable level. They make events seem expectable, even predictable and are ideally continuously adapted and reshaped to meet the requirements of the current situation.

This means that the inner world of an organization is controlled through reduction in complexity and that the organization controls itself through shared meanings, value structures and visions, through conventions, rituals and customs, through role allocation and organizational structures.

An organization is a multi-dimensional social system with its own inner world that really only exists through being a sub-system of larger systems in which it communicates and engages with other systems.

Systemic coaching and constellation

Since the mid-1990s, some coaches and organizational consultants have been using systemic coaching and constellations in large and small businesses to help establish flow and vitality in leadership and organizational life according to Whittington (2016). This systemic coaching approach is best understood through case studies where the methodology comes to life in the practice, which offers an opportunity to highlight, clarify and resolve system dynamics.

These dynamics are often invisible or unconscious to the client and through the process of being coached in this way, it opens the client to make contact with something that talking can rarely reach, which are often forces in systems that hide below the surface of symptoms, challenges or resistance.

Whittington (2016) defines a systemic constellation as a visible relational map of the client's invisible inner image of the relationship system. This image is, through a facilitated process, illuminated, disentangled and brought into better balance through the application of the insights, principles and practices of this work.

A systemic constellation allows the leader access to a living map where they can start to look at complex relationship systems in a manageable and respectful way. This approach can be useful for a leader when they want to work through a specific issue and want to delve deeper to literally stand in the system, which allows them to understand the hidden dynamics that can also include relationships and loyalties that are at play.

The coaching tools that are often used are: (1) flip chart page, (2) figures laid out on a tabletop or (3) sheets of paper located on a floor, any of which can be used to map out key elements represented in this issue or difficulty. Through contemplating each element, the leader can take a wider perspective on the relationship between the inter-related elements. This creates a deeper awareness for the leader where more options and realignment can emerge whereby changes can be created that bring about better flow and function.

John a leader who was interviewed for this research had experienced a systemic coaching session during his phase of transition and he described the experience whereby with tabletop figures

> the coach got me into using figures and bits of things and the coach asking where are you and where is everybody else and where do you want them to be?
>
> It was sort of very conceptual but I found it was huge as it brought up so many different opportunities or possibilities and I think that is the value of it. It was facilitated by the coach but it came from me.
>
> Certainly, the way this was done, more emerged perhaps rather than from a conversation because it is different . . . it was just those kinds of questions, where are you in relation to this group and it is natural in terms of . . . but if someone had said to me think about this. It was just . . . I wouldn't have been able to match that.

This is also a place where the leader can consider their own strengths, limitations, responsibilities and entanglements in the system. And from here the leader has a new inner map of the situation they were dealing with and can reach their own felt sense of place in the system.

It is important to note that the coach who facilitates a systemic constellation calls on their own presence and maturity as a person. Equally, it calls on their personal and professional experience in this area of coaching work and ideally have done a certain amount of work on themselves and have explored their own issues and have a heightened awareness of their own systemic associations.

Organizational politics

The idea of a leader being political may have negative connotations. Yet in reality political skill is a necessity for leaders and is a positive skill to possess when used appropriately. When political skill is viewed from this lens, it is difficult to envision any leader being effective without it and it can be very much linked to career success.

In general, organizational politics is often defined as the behaviour that is aimed at safeguarding the self-interest of an individual at the cost of another. Organizational politics can also be recognized in informal group settings, which often reside in the workplace where various types of associations or affiliations have a tendency to develop among individuals. These types of settings can either be encouraged or weakened by the organizational cultural values and the path they will take.

Organizational life has changed with the demise of the more traditional structure where hierarchical rules abound and the environment is a stable and predictable world of work. In today's VUCCA (Volatility, Uncertainty, Complexity, Chaos and Ambiguity) world and in the twenty-first century, organizations have more fluidity, uncertainty and ambiguity than ever before.

With the revival after the financial crisis of 2008 along with global trade negotiations and geopolitical landscape, much has changed as to the speed of organizational life. To this end also the nature of organizations has changed and how they are resourced in terms of the development of partnerships and joint ventures, sub-contracting, outsourcing, the gig economy and virtual teams working over multiple locations.

More recently with the outbreak of the COVID-19 global health pandemic, many organizations had to quickly prepare their workers to work from home through the use of technology. So why would a leader need to consider their own political power or their allies? Whereas in the past hierarchy and status commanded control, today expert power that is reflected in those who understand the key issues will take the decisions regardless of job title and status.

So, in many cases, this will not be the senior leader. This is a more fluid power and relies on the person's own personal and interpersonal resources and therefore these political skills can be used to advance their personal and organizational agenda. So senior leaders need to develop their own strategies in an ethical way to influence both within and outside of the organization.

For leaders in transition, the development of a stakeholder plan is often a useful exercise to undertake and they can decide who they need to collaborate and align with to get things done around here, which supports them in achieving their personal and organizational agenda. The senior leader needs to develop opportunities to build relationships with key stakeholders as early as possible.

Personal brand and identity

Personal brand is an important consideration for a leader in transition. Trust and credibility are cornerstones of brand. Companies are well known to value the concept of brand. When a company's brand gets damaged, it impacts on shareholders, customers and employees. When it comes to organizational life, leaders need to earn the trust and partnership of their employees and other stakeholders who look to them for direction and never more so than when things become unstable or there are doubts. So, trust is key. For new leaders who have been selected, their arrival creates expectations.

So, what leaders want to be known for can become their brand, whether that be their area of expertise, how they build relationships and their general visibility, along with the communications style and mediums they use. For leaders coming with much technical expertise, it is important that as they progress into more senior leadership roles they can also make that progression from relying on their expertise to also being an effective communicator.

As quoted by Warren Buffett, 'It takes 20 years to build a reputation and five minutes to ruin it' (Berman 2014: 1). For leaders in transition a coach could explore the leader's personal values with them and get them to consider the type of leader they want to be at this time.

Culture change leadership transition

Bridges and Mitchell (2002) discuss new models of change, where managing change is critical to the leader's success. They emphasize that change should be appropriate to a modern, fast-moving organization, where work is distributed among contributors both inside and outside of one's organization: work that is based on task and meaning, rather than job description.

It is not a control and command style of leadership appropriate to yesterday's organization; rather, it is the give and take, person-centred leadership by which the sports coach gets the best effort out of each member of the team. They cite that the best leadership development solutions implicitly address the challenge of understanding change – they are experiential, tailored to the needs of the leader, and based on delivering real-world results. But most could be strengthened by explicit attention to transition management.

When arriving at a company that has a long history, it will have had leaders who have left their own legacies over the years along with established ways of doing things. Therefore, it is likely that a certain type of thinking and behaviour is likely ingrained in the corporate culture.

McKinsey, a management consultancy organization, described culture as 'the way we do things around here', a phrase that is challenged by Schein (Kuppler 2015: 1). So, the leaders' understanding of the current culture needs to be considered as they transition into a new role, as it may be significantly different from where they have moved. While leaders who are transitioning to a new role start to experience how business gets carried out on a daily basis, part of their remit may also be to lead small- or large-scale change and transformation initiatives.

That term 'culture eats strategy for breakfast' is a quote often attributed to management consultant and writer, Peter Drucker (Campbell, Edgar and Stonehouse 2011: 263). The impact of culture on a company's strategy is only as effective as the strategy is solid in the first place. This also relates to the values that are the invisible force of the organization. While strategy is important, a culture that is strong and empowering can have a significant influence on productivity, engagement and innovation.

Change ultimately calls for adaptation and new ways of doing things. Here leaders need to consider the impact of change on the teams and other stakeholders who will be impacted by the change. So again, leaders know what they know, and can consider what they don't know while also stepping into the unknown unknown.

Leadership personal style and values will influence culture to a point but culture is very much a group phenomenon. Behavioural change, through building new habits and adapting to new routines, takes mental effort and only over time can the desired change be embedded. Change is not an event but a transition to a new way of being so continued effort is needed before it feels like the new normal.

Culture

Johnson, Whittington and Scholes (2012) identified six inter-related elements that make up culture. Those elements include Stories, Rituals and Routines, Symbols, Organizational Structure, Control Systems and Power Structures. They didn't try and identify any one best culture but they argued that by analysing each element a leader can decide if the current approach in the organization helps to deliver the vision and mission or hinder it.

Culture is a culmination of all of these elements and how they interconnect. You may have heard it referred to as the culture paradigm. Johnston, Whittington and Scholes call this 'the paradigm' or 'the recipe' – the summary of how these elements interconnect.

Leaders that are new to the business need to get an understanding of the overall culture and also the multiple cultures that are embedded within the organization and then consider any shifts that are required to improve performance. Business results would be one of the most common culture styles in organizations. Building shareholder value is always on the agenda. Culture shapes attitudes and behaviours and cultural norms define what is encouraged or discouraged, accepted or rejected within a group.

Leaders are the catalysts who define an aspirational target culture and develop strategies to achieve the desired culture. Friction is often evident in times of change and the leader's authority is not always the means to achieving the change. So, leaders do need to consider how best they can influence the culture change and sometimes this can be an uncomfortable place for them.

Equally, the leader can overplay their dominant presence through authority where they try and force the culture change, which can result in resistance or they may find that the culture is only partially embedded over time. Even though culture change is often managed through a project management approach, the embedding of real and sustainable change can only happen through mindset shifts and behavioural change that comes about through understanding and embracing the reason for change which needs to be seen in action

The need for the change needs to be constantly communicated by the leader. Culture is like the breath of an organization and is something that a leader in transition will see and feel as they navigate their way on a daily basis.

Leadership in a virtual environment

For leaders new to a business who have never met face-to-face and are working with their team for the first time virtually, it will be especially hard to develop social cohesion. Members of virtual teams need to rely more on trust to work together effectively than in face-to-face teams. This is worth bearing in mind for new leaders who won't always have the benefit of pre-existing relationships.

Social cohesion and relationship-building are key components of building trust, which can be harder to develop in virtual teams because communication through electronic media reduces the social cues required to build relationships. Separately working across time zones in globally dispersed organizations makes synchronization more difficult, so leaders need to focus on building deliberate awareness of the optimal time intervals for meetings.

Trusting each other means team members can suspend their judgement about others and prevent potential misunderstandings and conflicts that are more likely to occur in virtual teams, where electronic media makes communication poorer and more difficult. Virtual teams can tend to focus on sharing what is strictly related to solving the problem or task at hand.

The new leader will need to consider ways of connecting the team and discuss and find ways of working together and connecting the team on a social level. Equally, team members need to know someone is listening to what they are saying and that their input counts and it is not just a one-way street or that the loudest person is heard. This will be important to the performance of the overall team.

Q.1 What might be an effective way to build social cohesion and relationships early with your team members?

Q.2 What has been the way or culture built up around communicating with the team before now?

Q.3 No matter how small the office or how far away you are from the organization's HQ, how can you as leader communicate to your direct reports and ultimately to your wider team members that their contribution is valued and that they will be supported?

Q.4 How will you know when you have built up trust with the team?

Why adopt a coaching style of leadership

In his studies on leadership, Daniel Goleman (2000) has identified six different leadership styles, one of which is coaching. The traditional role of the leader has been shifting from control and command and this change has been significantly influenced by a workforce of knowledge workers, work structures and the onset of digital transformation across organizations.

As the structure of work involves more teams-based work on projects and the work environment has been rapidly moving to virtual working, there has been a fundamental shift in terms of the skills and behaviour that are now required of leaders. No longer can a leader assume followership purely from the basis of authority and power. Many leaders today are learning the skill of coaching and they have ongoing conversations as they engage with team members around business deliverables.

John, a leader who participated in the research, spoke about his experience on acquiring coaching skills.

I have done the Coaching Diploma and I coach people internally and externally. So now I have much more of an idea of what coaching is and the potential benefits of it.

But I am also at this point because I am doing coaching, I am also doing coaching supervision so there is that element as well. But that is different, that is very much focusing on the coaching experience. My current coaching arrangement is around the transition and the impact I will have in my new directorate.

As with situational leadership, the leader's ability to adapt their style to the situation is valuable. More and more leaders are moving towards adopting a coaching style of leadership and the phrase comes to mind 'he who creates the solution, owns the solution'. A coaching style allows the leader to pose questions that can elicit clarity of a situation, consider options and decide on a way forward. This approach also enables the development of the team member and leads towards more self-sufficiency with autonomy and personal growth.

Developing a roadmap – first 100 days

A roadmap is an effective way to consider and plan out the way forward as the leader starts to perform in the new role and a coach can offer such support as they work with the new leader.

According to Bossert (2005), the function of the roadmap is to help the newcomers navigate the challenge of making the transition, along with navigating the organizational structure, business strategy and organizational culture in order to accelerate productivity. Bossert also considers as equally important the new leader's own personality traits, leadership style and professional skills and capability, which must also be considered.

He goes on to recommend that the remainder of the transition plan should map out key actions to be carried out within the first 100 days, in order to position the leader and his or her team for long-term success. So, in effect, the new leader is given time to think through the changes that are emerging.

Depending on company culture and policy around on-boarding a leader new to their role, they may be assigned a mentor or peer or an internal coach to get acquainted with the organization. Either way, the leader can also decide to navigate the transition through informal meetings with colleagues within the business or seek the support of a trusted colleague or request the services of an in-house resource or external resource, so there are many options available to the leader.

In terms of internal resources available to the leader, any of these options can be a pathway to start to learn about culture 'how we do things around here', gain insight into current strategic projects, perceived challenges and opportunities, who the key influencers are, key stakeholders (internal and external) and the style of leadership and political nuances.

External coaches can bring an external perspective along with a sense of confidentiality and psychological safety, perhaps that is not always perceived to be available in other work-related relationships.

This conversational space allows the leader to explore the new territory and may over time show some vulnerability, which they may not otherwise wish to show as they step into their new leadership role. Times of change can often bring a dip in confidence and a sense of aloneness even for the most seasoned leaders. So a trusting confidante is a gift of sorts for a new leader in a world that is fast paced and competitive.

Tripartite meeting

When an organization arranges for the leader to be matched with a coach, the organization becomes a vested party. More often than not, an initial three-way meeting with the new leader and their senior leader along with the coach will be arranged to discuss expectations and a timeline for the coaching to take place.

New coaches may be curious as to what coaching techniques to apply and how to apply them. In many ways the answer to this question is shaped by the context of the coaching and the agreements reached between the client organization and the coach. If a three-way meeting takes place between the coach, new leader and senior leader, the outcome of the discussion will influence the direction for the coaching intervention.

Tripartite coaching assignment

Name of coachee:

High-level goal / objective: _____

_____

_____

_____

Desirable result / outcomes(s): _____

_____

_____

_____

Measures of success:

_____

_____

_____

Start date: _____

Review date: (if agreed): _____

Completion date: _____

No. of sessions agreed: _____

Signed by: *Date:* _____

Coachee: _____

Coachee's manager: _____

Coach: _____

Evaluating the coaching investment

In the evaluation of the coaching section of the 6th Ridler Report (Mann 2016: 19) 'return on expectations' (RoE)) is the most commonly used measure for the investment made in coaching. This involves the coachee setting expectations for the coaching assignment in conjunction with their line manager and the coach at the outset. Three-way meetings according to this report are now clearly widely used. The outcomes of the coaching assignment are compared with the objectives at, or a few months after and/or the end of the assignment.

In terms of evaluation measures, organizations indicated the measures they currently use for evaluating the coaching intervention are:

74% – subjective evaluation against the individual's assignment coaching objectives
63% – testimonials of coachee
62% – coachee's satisfaction score
54% – coachee's line manager satisfaction score

Furthermore, what organizations would deem as valuable measures of evaluation for the coaching investment (if they were available) are:

87% – comparative 360-degree feedback pre and post coaching – currently 26% gathering this data*
85% – organizational insights emerging from the coaching – currently only 38% gathering this data
80% – financially based return on investment – currently 14% gathering this data
74% – a change in employee engagement scores – currently 22% gathering this data
* Note: it was noted that comparative 360-degree feedback pre and post coaching can be seen as time-consuming for the coachee's colleagues and those coordinating the 360-degree feedback.

5 Research on leaders' experience of the impact of coaching

The research study sought to create a framework for understanding the impact of coaching on leaders as they transition into a new role. This study qualitatively explored senior leaders' perspectives from both the private and public sectors.

Eight senior leaders (five males and three females), all from large organizations in Ireland, were interviewed in 2017 as part of this study. Data from this sample were collected using semi-structured interviews. The data were analysed using thematic analysis. Pseudonym names have been used for reasons of confidentiality.

Leaders No. 1 to No. 7 were promoted within the organizations they already worked in. Leader No. 8 moved to a new organization when he took on the leadership role.

Leaders' experience of the impact of coaching

Each of the eight leaders shared their experience of working with a coach and discussed the impact the coaching had for them.

Table 5.1 **Participant profile** (pseudonyms are used for participants)

Participant No.	Role	Gender	Name	Length of time in leadership roles (years)
No. 1	Head of Function	F	Helena	20
No. 2	Head of Function	M	Jim	5
No. 3	Head of Function	F	Kate	5
No. 4	Head of Function	M	Kevin	20
No. 5	Head of Function	M	John	6
No. 6	Global Director	M	Paul	20
No. 7	Global Head of Function	F	Marion	4
No. 8	Head of Function	M	Richard	5

Helena (No. 1)

Helena has held a number of leadership roles for almost 20 years with varying degrees of responsibility. More recently, Helena has taken on a new senior leadership role as head of an IT function in a large organization where she has held leadership roles of varying responsibility previously. In her new role, she has nine direct reports who lead 300 employees in the overall function.

She has experienced coaching previously, always when moving into more senior roles and she acknowledges those as positive experiences where she has learned a lot, mainly about herself. She has become a coach herself within the organization, which brings a whole other dimension.

On this occasion, Helena requested a coach through the L&D (Learning & Development) function and selected an external coach for her latest senior leadership role because of the people dimension and she wanted the opportunity to self-assess. She undertook 6×1.5hr coaching sessions, which stretched out over an eight-month timeframe while she was transitioning into the new senior leadership role.

Helena selected the coach and over that first chemistry meeting she gelled with the coach fairly quickly because she felt they both were quite open and understood the coaching process. Helena held a clear view as to what she would like to achieve and they started the meeting with a discussion around what the key challenges were and where Helena saw herself. Helena started outlining key goals that she wanted to achieve through the coaching. They also agreed how often they would meet, dates were pre-set and Helena's manager was involved later in a tripartite meeting.

Helena acknowledged the vast amount of change the organization was going through and the role she now holds saw five different senior leaders move through it in the past two years. She notes that the team have experienced a level of change that is probably too much. The biggest challenge she sees is a huge challenge from the people side because of the level of uncertainty and change.

While being coached, Helena acknowledged a number of areas that coaching enabled some breakthrough for her when she was transitioning to a new role in areas such as creating *discipline around reflection, planning, identifying value add, immediate and future focus* and *delivering results*.

> It is not just about the coaching meeting, what it does is that it instils that discipline in you – every day I take a half an hour now where I just sit and I just reflect myself around my plans or what I have done or how I am feeling. It just instils that discipline.

> I looked at where I could bring the value now, where I am now, where I wanted to be in the future, but where I can hit the ground running and where I can bring value while I plan and bring my team on board to develop a plan for the future . . . coaching allowed me to take time out to deliver the results so there is an end game in mind.

I would see working with a coach as a hugely enriching experience and anyone in my view to think that it is taking time away from you is foolish,
because what it does is, it creates so much value in other ways. It just creates some other avenues for you and it creates that space for you which is
kind of invaluable really.

Some of the ways that coaching works for Helena is through having her *thinking and assumptions challenged* while also *objectively analysing her
own and others' behaviours and situations that emerge.* This enables the
leader to widen their lens with critical thinking to explore challenges and
opportunities.

> . . . and the opportunity to explore your own thinking and to have somebody
> challenge that thinking in a very non . . . in a very kind of different way, but
> I suppose for me it really is giving me that time to stand back and reflect and
> look at myself, my behaviours, look at situations and others' behaviours and
> I suppose very objectively analyse myself as well but giving me the space to
> do that because in a very busy world it is extremely difficult to do that.

> Value add, huge value add. And directional I would say in the context I sup-
> pose of, in a traditional way, she is not coming up with all the answers for
> me. She is just kind of challenging some of your assumptions and mainly
> thinking about possible ways forward for you and you come up with that
> together. So yes, directional and value add.

> So, I think absolutely all the coaching experience, all the questioning and
> listening and when I say challenging, I mean, just saying, you know, let me
> be the devil's advocate and play the devil's advocate. And then when a deci-
> sion needs to be made, make the decision, call it, move on, be consistent
> and be true to yourself as well . And sometimes they are not the easiest by
> any stretch of the imagination and they do take a lot of time and energy.
> I mean it's exhausting work but so worthwhile.

Coaching also created space to develop *vision and direction* that would
inspire followership.

> Also setting out the long-term vision and creating that vision for people and
> getting the energy or having or bringing the energy I should say, that people
> get excited or enthused about getting on the bus with you.

Feeling psychologically safe is critical to the success of a coaching relationship and Helena notes it needs to be a *two-way process* to get the most
out of it

> It has to be a two-way thing. You have to be able to put your soul on the table
> and if you are feeling emotional and upset about something, you need to be
> able to share that and that needs to be a safe environment for you to do so.

So, if you don't completely have that relationship with your coach and you don't trust them enough, I don't think you are going to get what you need to get out of coaching.

The coaching sessions enabled *clarity of thought* and allowed a *sense of structure*, which helped Helena *identify priorities* and *develop a plan*

The opportunity to create clarity of thought and now as I move into the middle it is about putting structure around that.

There is so much to be done. There are a million priorities. It helped me to see the woods from the trees and attend to the important versus the unimportant and to compartmentalize things and to focus on your short, medium and long term.

I suppose what it created for me was the ability to pause for thought, to look at things differently, to look at them from different perspectives.

Coaching sessions provided Helena with a *check-in* point to *review* and *revise* where she was as she transitioned into the role. While it is important for a leader to collaborate and seek inputs from stakeholders and team members, it is also important to step out of the action and reflect at stages. Organizations are systems with people who have differing needs and perspectives, so there are often multiple dynamics at play. All the more reason for a leader to be able to *step back* and *objectively reflect* on their position at a given time to ensure they are moving in the direction they intended.

Am I looking at this the right way and you are trying to listen to everybody. You could get the whole thing derailed and with the coaching, it helps you to stand back and realize where you are and then go back and . . . what I set out at the beginning is where I am now, where I wanted to be in three to six months' time, where I wanted to be in a year's time or whatever and how . . . or am I moving further and further away and what adjustments do I have to make. Do I have to expedite things? Are there individuals I have to work with? Do I have to do something off line? Do I have to seek . . . from the rest of the SMT?

Helena explored how she could *maintain her energy levels* and *stay resilient* for the weeks and months ahead. Even the most resilient leaders while they may feel resilient themselves, need to consider the resilience of others. If they overplay their own resilience, this can have an adverse effect on some of their team members who may not be as resilient and it could lead to overwhelm or stress in the team. So being mindful of resilience and what that might look like for the leader and the team is important. In today's VUCCA world, resilience has nearly become a pre-requisite skill for senior leaders.

Again, it can be very impactful when this is all great and energized but how do you maintain it? How do you stay resilient, how do you keep that energy going and I think that is where coaching comes into its own as well?

Senior leaders are leaders of other leaders and the *influence of leadership* cascades throughout the organization. For Helena, while acknowledging the individual leaders who reported to her as they have their individual responsibilities for the business functions they lead, she also wanted to create a team dynamic that supported a common vision. It was important for Helena to have all of her *leadership team working together* and to *enable empowerment* and for *success to be shared.*

Here, Helena also reflected on the style of the senior leaders who had been in the role before her. She was the fifth senior leader to lead this team in a two-year period so there had been much transitioning for the team as well as their new senior leader. Helena is also aware that when the going gets tough or times become uncertain, teams tend to look to their leaders for guidance and the leader is left to find a way forward with the support of others or not. Either way, the leader must ultimately navigate a way forward and bring the team with them through whatever change they face.

> I also want to bring them together as a management team. I want them to be seen as such. I want them to shine and I want them to feel that they are completely empowered and that's all nice language but that's actually what needs to happen as well so that they can be successful because this isn't about me. It's about them because they are the real leaders of the next layer down and so on.

> I want to bring my team on board to develop a plan for the future.

> How can you bring them together in one unit with such strength, power and you know with their own clarity of thought but I suppose lack of leadership, is what they were really missing, you know.

> You know there are different ways of solving things like bringing people together, it's about empowering others. It's about helping you to be a great leader in that context and I think that's where coaching comes into its own. You don't have to do all the things.

> You just have to be the voice of reason when everything else is falling apart and you just have to be as you say authentic and you have to be, you know, I suppose, clear and you have to be really authentic and you have to bring people with you and you also have to let people have the freedom to be creative and all of those things.

> People do look to you, they do, when they get doubts in their head is when you really have to and when the going gets tough, that's when you really have to stay true to yourself.

Effective interactions and *communication* are key to engaging with others. *Collaborating with others* and *building new relationships* with the team and other stakeholders is important for the new leader. Even more so in today's world, when senior leaders need to rely more than ever on their influence and followership. No longer is followership gained by the traditional leadership style of power and control. Now more than ever, each leader needs to earn trust and credibility to ensure others will both follow and support the business agenda.

> I see the challenges that there are and I also see the opportunities and I talk in a language of opportunity and motivation rather than challenge and issues.
>
> . . . and also to invest in people and to try things and let them fail. So, what, like? What you have done is that you have built a relationship.
>
> We are one part of the organization but we are also part of one organization and, yes, developing the relationships, as it is all about relationships and people.
>
> So, I suppose I put a huge emphasis on relationships. I always would have had but I think the value of them and how easy they are to damage and how precious they are and how hard they are to build back up.

Sourcing feedback for personal stretch and growth is a hallmark of *leadership development*. There are many tools available and for Helena the 360-degree assessment provided valuable feedback from a number of sources.

> Well there's loads of different tools. Well one of the things I always finds beneficial anyway is the 360 because that's a real reflection back to you about how people are feeling about you.

Empowering others and *fostering autonomy* in others helps *develop others potential*.

> It's not about solving everything . . . you know there are different ways of solving things like bringing people together, it's about empowering others. It's about helping you to be a great leader in that context and I think that's where coaching comes into its own. You don't have to do all the things, do you know what I mean?
>
> I suppose what coaching created for me was an opportunity to be the best that I can be so that I can actually enjoy creating opportunities for others to be the best that they can be. And I think that actually is that and it is not all about the job with me. It's actually about helping others realize their potential and to create the environment for them to shine. And I think that for me and coaching actually helped me to realize that about myself. And I might have missed that completely.

On wider reflection, while considering the overall impact of the coaching, Helena *reflected on her own traits, strengths and motivation as a leader*. She became *aware of how her own unique leadership style and motivations*, all of which enable her to create a positive work environment, were key ingredients to enable people to want to be a part of her team. And that in itself was *acknowledgement of the impact of her leadership style*, which was a powerfully developmental aspect of the coaching.

> I suppose this is one of the things where coaching helped me . . . you know, I suppose all my life I have always been a very driven person and, you know, delivering results would have been very important to me and I suppose I am very hard on myself and I suppose what coaching made me appreciate was the talents I could bring to the table as well and how you can bring people with you.
>
> So, I suppose one of my strengths that I discovered or a by-product which I really didn't think I had before was the strong leadership skills that I have, the ability I have to create the environment for people, in a psychological safe environment where people can speak openly, where we can plan together and there is no such thing as a wrong suggestion.
>
> Also, setting out the long-term vision and creating that vision for people and getting the energy or having or bringing the energy I should say, that people get excited and enthused about getting on the bus with you.
>
> And then I suppose and it's not something I ever realized I did or that I do quite naturally because, you know, when I take on a role or whatever, I just take it on. I see the challenges that they are and I also see the opportunities and I talk in a language of opportunity and motivation rather than challenge and issues because you know they are all there, of course they are, but behind every challenge is an opportunity and it is about creating that kind of space for people to feel, yes, gosh yes, somebody has our back, oh yes, I can make that suggestion. That they lose their fear and therefore the skills and the talent they have, you really unleash them. And creating that enthusiasm and energy.
>
> Like yes, of course I am a good organizer and a good worker and yes all of those good things that you would expect but it is that kind of, what I see as and I haven't seen before, is that I do see the big picture and I can stand up and I am not afraid to say I don't have all the answers. I need help here, you are my team. Do you know what I mean? You create that environment that everybody wants to be a part of and get quite excited about it and I get quite excited, thrilled.

Jim (No. 2)

Jim has held leadership roles for the past five years. In his previous senior leadership role he didn't have direct reports as his work was externally focused where he influenced and engaged with external peers. In his latest appointment to Head of Function in the area of Finance, he has both an internal and external focus and he has six direct reports and an overall team of 30.

This move takes Jim away from his previous area of expertise to a different part of the organization. It's a different landscape and a different time career wise and while he is not quite sure where his next career move might be, he has career planning needs he want to consider too.

Jim has had a previous positive experience of working with a coach and this time around he requested a coach via L&D and sought to work with an external coach because of his career stage. He also wanted to work with a coach who was more attuned to the psychological aspects of behaviour and different personalities so that he could gain some insight to apply within his own approach to managing and leading. Jim's senior leader is very supportive of the coaching and has engaged in a tripartite meeting with a view to how they will work together over the first three months or 100 days.

Jim found the *coaching questions helpful when he was in the 'not knowing' stage,* either about the role or what the future holds for his career beyond this role. *Through timeout to reflect, his thinking evolved* about himself and the role.

> So it was quite a different role. Both in terms of the shape of the team and the size of the team.
>
> Probably not knowing the role as well is the core thing and also being at a stage of my career development where I am not quite sure of what I am going to do next.
>
> It's a different landscape and also it's a different time career wise.
>
> So they are the kind of things that definitely evolved and making me think myself about how I think about the role and what is in the role.

Jim acknowledges the *value of taking time out and reflecting* in his very busy role. He has seen the value of *freeing up time to think and plan* and during this time *he thinks about his engagement with others, which he now sees as very valuable for him.*

> Just . . . taking time away . . . making time away from day to day work to think about how you can progress to be a better leader in your role and that is something I value very much. I have a very busy role as such as there is a lot going on and I can very easily get caught up with meetings and tasks and all of that. So, I think getting into coaching gives me a very good . . . it's almost a good bit of time and it is a constant reminder to focus on that development of potential and growth and to maybe think about things that are in the back of my head or in the middle of my head and know that I should be doing. It brings me back to what I should be doing this day, this week. It keeps me honest to myself.
>
> I was very much focused on tasks and deliverables and deadlines and that was important in the role as well, but coaching did it to some extent the first time and it is definitely doing it again this time. It is making me realize the benefit and freeing myself up from the day to day, to spend a bit of time reflecting and considering things and planning how to engage with people before I do and to see that there is huge merit in that, and

that is not me taking time out sitting about blue-sky gazing. That is incredibly useful.

Jim noted that questions from the coach **challenged his thinking** while also **helping him become accountable to himself.**

What I liked about it the first time was what the coach did. It's like putting up the mirror to you and asking you the questions that you are asking yourself and maybe not verbalizing them and asking them explicitly and I like the fact that it made me be more accountable to myself.

From the beginning, the coaching allowed Jim **to step back** and **think strategically** to **get clarity around a vision** while he also **developed a plan to make it all happen.** The approach allowed Jim to get explicit clarity by writing out what he wanted to have happen in a year's time.

At the beginning, I think it was very much getting me to sit back and think strategically about where I wanted to be, so we did this exercise taking a helicopter view of where I wanted to be in 12 months and again it explicitly made me sit down and say what exactly do I want things to look like. And then put steps in place to follow and to get there. So, the beginning was very much making that time to picture that vision.

Jim was conscious of the **impact of his communication style** and his way of **engaging with his new team.**

I guess I have a natural interest in how my words and actions impacted on those around me and the different personalities and the psychology of those people within the team

All the more important that you be a very good listener and be able to engage with people quite well.

Gaining clarity was key for Jim at a time when he had moved into a new business area and was now busy juggling a lot of different things as he navigated the transition. So **figuring out and refining what he wanted to achieve** was very important at the start. After that he could plan a way forward.

I think I could go back to that and that was really what I wanted at the start and I think there was clarity in that and this time around again probably getting to that stage of clarity this is now what I want out of this, I want this out of this engagement which would have taken a bit more work and that is fine with me because I knew I was throwing a lot of balls in the air, so the clarity at the beginning – whether that comes in the 1st session or the 3rd session – I think is one of the most beneficial aspects of it. After that it is a bit of . . . well, what are the steps to get to and do the steps whereas I think the hardest part is figuring out what I want at the end.

As the coaching progressed it *allowed opportunities to review and revise the plan* and *see the picture that Jim did achieve* even better than he initially thought he would.

> and the middle was how are we progressing, how can we shift things to focus around a little bit better to see how we can make it happen and at the end it gave me a great sense of satisfaction and achievement and validation of the value of the coaching. I could see the picture that I wanted and I absolutely got there and I even did it a bit better.

Jim considers *the discipline of how he will work* and *how best to work with his team.* Confidence can dip in unknown territory and Jim is *finding confidence* in terms of *sorting out* what he can *let go* of to his team and *what he needs to focus on.*

> There is a danger a little bit of being I know it all and you know it all better yourself and moving to a team now where you don't know anyone's role.

> So, I think I can improve on that and I can definitely improve in being a bit more disciplined in how I work, as well in that I could be better to let people do the task themselves and stay totally out of it. But I think a certain amount of it will evolve more naturally. I am more confident with what is going on and I don't have to spend more time understanding everything so I can sort through what is the stuff I can let go and what do I need to be more on top of so they are a couple of things.

Jim wanted to work with a coach who was more attuned to psychological aspects. He had undertaken psychological assessments as part of the selection process and was interested to see how he could use this insight as a leader. He started *thinking about the role* and *what it means for him* and *how he can get to know the team members.* Also he considered *personality styles* and how best to *engage with the others* as he reflected on the *diversity of personalities.* Reflecting on his *own style, its impact* and how he can *adapt as he engages with others* and *build relationships,* Jim said:

> Others (coaches) were attuned to the more psychological aspects of it and that was more where I was leaning towards. I actually found through some of the work that was required for the interviews we did for senior manager tests, psychology is part of that and I found that really useful and really interesting. I suppose it's a part of managing or leading that I was always interested in.

> Making me think myself about how I think about the role and what is in the role and definitely this time more of a slant towards the people side and towards the psychology of all of it, the types of personalities that you are engaging with.

And, I guess, even now as I interact with the team I am engaging with now, I would have a good sense already of what general personality types they may be and some people are more transparent and some people are more guarded and I just need to interact with them the right way.

Especially when I started off in a position where I thought I was a good listener. I thought they knew where I was coming from. I probably did try but I didn't actually act on it. So, I think I can improve on that.

I am interested in people and I think as a manager and a leader of people that's a natural strength, because you are more inclined to think about where people are coming from and to think about how a change or a request or a task might be interpreted by someone, because I am more recently promoted and have come through the ranks, so I am also more probably aware as to . . .

There are certain real high achievers on my team and they want to get promoted themselves and I have a personal understanding where people are at in their lives and so I think a strength might be trying to understand where people are coming from and spending time considering that when I am trying to engage and work with them. So that aspect of relationship building is important to me.

Definitely in the first coaching experience the time we spent initially thinking about where people were coming from, as I managed six people at that time from slightly varying backgrounds. Spending much more time thinking how they interacted with me at the start was very beneficial.

As Jim takes time to consider stakeholders he *realizes the large number of stakeholders* he has in the new role and *considers some key relationships* he will need to build, he is also aware that he cannot take *relationships with his own team* for granted. *Building relationships with many different stakeholders* will be a key part of Jim's new role

I probably had an early focus on relationships within the team but I didn't see the full opportunity in that from the start. Opportunities in probably really understanding that stakeholder map and as I am only getting into that now, understanding what are the interactions, how often I should do them, how they will be different with different people.

We probably have a much bigger number, much bigger than I thought. There's a lot of stakeholders in this particular job. Even the amount of stakeholders internally in this part of the business alone: I didn't have a sense of before I went in.

It has probably opened my eyes a bit to that and also maybe just pointing me back towards both relationships with those key relationships with my team and not taking any of that for granted.

Another thing I would like to do is to be more focused actively building relationships with stakeholders.

Jim realizes the *value of feedback* and decides to be *more disciplined* in terms of *improving his listening skills*

> Even just feedback and I guess understanding the psychometrics helped towards pushing me down that road anyway. Especially when I started off in a position where I thought I was a good listener. I thought they knew where I was coming from. I probably did try but I didn't actually act on it. So, I think I can improve on that and I can definitely improve in being a bit more disciplined in how I work as well in that I could be better to let people do the task themselves and stay totally out of it. But I think a certain amount of it will evolve more naturally.
>
> And again I would say before I did the coaching I had good sense that I thought about it but I didn't put it into action half enough and the feedback from the psychometric definitely helped me to say, well look, you are not doing that enough, you need to focus more. You might well know, you think you know about it but unless you do it, you are not putting it into action. So, I think that was the core thing I got out of it.

Jim's *confidence has grown* in terms of what he *can now let go* of and *how much he needs to know* in order to *feel on top of things*. Also, Jim has taken the *opportunity to develop* and is more *self-aware* in terms of *his engagement style, developmental areas*, his *purpose, direction* and *values*.

> Now that I am six months into the role, I am more confident with what is going on and I don't have to spend more time understanding everything so I can sort through what is the stuff I can let go and what do I need to be more on top of so they are a couple of things.
>
> Self-awareness mostly of myself but also of other people and the things like listening and empathy that all come from that relationship but the thing about where if someone wants to work with you, you will get somewhere faster and better and understanding where they are and where you are. To me that all wraps into and just as I am speaking, it is coming to me that awareness of self and that awareness of the other person probably and that idea of purpose and direction and values. All that intangible that isn't, let's say, at the front of our brain. It does more of that gut and sleeping on it. That is coming out for me more, which I am delighted about.

Jim also considered a *career path going forward* and *articulated his ambitions for the future*. He has *started visualizing* and *considered what the next level of senior leadership* might need as he thought of role models that he could refer to.

> How is this going to pan out now that I am in my late 30s compared to when I was in my 20s? I was going to plan out where I am going to be in the next five or six years . . . where am I going to be at the end of it. So, there are

bigger strategic questions, if you like, around career as well. So that made it a bit harder to put a picture on what I want exactly out of the coaching.

And I have ambitions to be a more senior leader and if the likes of X who is executive director and other directors, they don't deliver themselves, they deliver through people.

I could see the picture that I wanted and I absolutely got there and I even did it a bit better and I learnt lots of . . . quite a bit along the way about personalities in the team that I was managing and I engaged with them and I felt that they had grown with me as I had kind of used these tools so that gave me a real sense of the value of coaching.

Kate (No. 3)

Kate had made a lateral career move leading a large-scale project within the organization, when she started working with an external coach. The coaching focus included key aspects of her work and also with a view to securing a further promotional role-change to senior leader, which she successfully achieved. She has previously worked in leadership roles for five years. Kate had just started in her new leadership role before going on maternity leave.

On her return from leave, almost a year later, she is finding her way in the new role and has picked up with the coach again as she works through the transition where much has changed within the industry during that time. Her latest role is Head of Function in the area of regulation across the commercial business sector. Her team have a high level of interaction with other external regulatory bodies and the function has a supervisory remit within the specific industry she works in.

Transition for Kate has been incremental from the time she moved to the role for a number of weeks and now returning from maternity leave with significant changes having taken place in the interim. The coaching was a bridge between the early stage of moving into the role and is now picked up again after a number of months. For Kate she was *finding her way in the role and at the more senior level and dealing with a lot of change*.

We were quite clear in terms of what we were trying to work on and then I was at that point adjusting to a new role even at that level.

I met her [coach] about six weeks after I started so I came back at the end of June and I met her through the middle of August. August would be a traditionally quiet month here and I would feel that a lot of . . . still really trying to find my feet in terms of the role.

The dynamic between ourselves and the regulated entities and the policy makers had changed significantly so it was dealing with a different dynamic as well. So, we were kind of finding our feet in terms of that new dynamic.

I just had to ensure the whole new dynamic was working effectively and it didn't become a problem and ensure there was an escalation of the key issues.

The coach has a way of challenging some of Kate's statements and assumptions in a ways that helps Kate *think through the issue*, which brings *unexpected results*.

> There is a challenge from her to me which I find helpful in the context of, you know, certain assumptions or statements that I would make . . . just for me to check those. So, she would say to me, so why do you think that? Or have you done any work around that? And maybe I would go . . . em . . . no, probably I haven't, so she actually gets me to challenge my own assumptions around maybe – perceived roadblocks is too strong a word – so I would say perceived just things I feel I would have to work my way around, whereas actually if I challenged that assumption it is not a big . . . I don't have to work my way around it . . . I can just go through it if that makes sense. Isn't that a strange thing probably to say . . . ? So, I find she has a very good way of just challenging some of the things that I am saying.

Kate acknowledges how she finds coaching creates a *safe environment*, which is not always readily available in organizations because of the nature of the system and hierarchical structure.

> Yes definitely. It's a very safe environment.

Kate finds the *downloading of information* helpful to *put structure on things*. This helps her to *get clear on issues, get rid of noise (distractions), analyse* and *identify specific areas to progress* with at each session. So it *brings focus*, which *gives Kate a sense of direction*. She finds that this is very helpful and *adds value*.

> And I think the coach is very good at structuring what the issues are because sometimes I just download a lot of information to the coach and then sometimes I can put some structure on it in terms of there are three things I want to discuss with you and I have probably found that as I have done more and more coaching, I am much more of, this is what I want to get out of this session, but initially I probably felt that it was downloading a lot of stuff and she would put some structure in terms of OK, well, I think that is related to that and this is the area we need to think about, maybe you would think about working on.

> Yes, directional and value add and I found it very structured and both my experiences with the coaches, what I find is amazing is when you do that download, so as I said I have got more structured in terms of how I should go with these three areas I think I should talk to you about today. I find coaches great in the context of you can do that download. It's amazing at the end of the session they have managed to deal with all of those things. They are thinking all the time in the context of all of that, maybe, noise and how we might kind of deal with that. I am always very surprised by that, like that is amazing, like they can tick off all of those things. Yeah, so that's very good.

Kate finds that when she is *working through issues*, it is helpful to have an *objective perspective that she can take learnings from* and helps *broaden her perspective*.

> You know so, in the first instance I would find having an objective perspective on the issues you are struggling with or need some guidance on very helpful.
>
> What I would say also is that I set very high standards for myself so that is good probably if you are my boss erm . . . but sometimes it might not be great if you are working with me so, sometimes good is good enough from that perspective so I think I have got to learn that that might not be exactly how I would do things.
>
> As I am settling more into the role, I am kind of seven months in it now, like new things are arising for me that we are discussing and I always get her perspective on those as well. It's not about revisiting the same old issues. So, the last session was three new things.

Kate found the coaching helpful in terms of reflecting on what she *needs to stop doing* and to consider what she can do and *what behaviours she needs to consider* to *have the desired impact* at the level of senior leader that she sees as *part of her own growth and development*. She sees this as an *intrinsic behavioural change* rather than an external change she needs to make. Kate realizes the importance of *understanding the business*, *acting strategically*, *adapting her communication message* and *acting on feedback she is already aware of*.

> So I found her very, very helpful in the context of just kind of, as you become more senior in the organization, how you stop doing the things you had done before because otherwise if you keep doing those, you are still operating at the same level and you are not growing and making sure you are really operating at the right level with your peers and the director and things like that.
>
> I think it is important to understand what are people talking about there, which is that I suppose to try and anticipate things a little bit more in advance and trying to raise it up a bit at the right level in that context with particular issues.
>
> So, I think you have to continue to work on that and also, I observe, so people I respect, people I have worked with previously, how they operate at committees in terms of their interventions and I suppose I have tried to learn from them in the context of how you interject when you want to make a point, what points you might make, what ones you might leave and, you know, things like that. So that is one aspect of it.
>
> Another piece of feedback I would have got as well is, in terms of my communication style, and this is something that I have been very conscious of is that not to be too elaborate in my communication and to be conscious of who my audience is. So more internally than externally, I think.

Kate reflected on the *use of her time*, which was a limited resource and also *her presence at meetings*. She was aware she needed to make that *shift from being the subject matter expert* with a focus on detail and prepare with *more focus and less detail* but feel adequately prepared for meetings.

> So I find the coach very helpful in the context of focusing your mind in terms of your presence in meetings. You have very little time to prepare how you might do that erm because before you would be in the detail because you are the subject matter expert in all of that kind of stuff.

Even though Kate feels she is quite structured, she *values talking through information*. Again, it is the download and it is an *opportunity to review and revise* the items she is working on.

> I am quite structured and organized but having said that, sometimes, I just find that the sessions that you just do a lot of talking initially and then we take a pause and then we just go back and revisit each of the items.

Kate realizes that as a leader she has limited capacity and needs to be *focused* and *work smart* and try and to *not get overwhelmed.* She also feels she can overplay her own *resilience* and that could have a negative impact on her team at times. With less time to undertake the detailed work, she now needs to *trust her team* and *let go and delegate* to *sustain her focus and energy*, *prepare efficiently*, *hold herself confidently* and *operate at the senior level.*

> I have also found her extremely beneficial in the context of . . . I think you know it's pretty important as you move up the organization, in terms of your capacity, so in terms of how you focus on the right things, how you can prepare efficiently for whatever is coming at you, how you ensure that your team is working efficiently and effectively and how you can ensure you are adding value and not get overwhelmed too much. So, I find her particularly beneficial in that context.

> I would say I am very resilient. I do have huge capacity, I think, and I sometimes think that can be a negative too. I can sometimes take that to the limit.

> Trusting your team, you know. So I found her very, very helpful in the context of just kind of, as you become more senior in the organization, how you stop doing the things you had done before. Because, otherwise, if you keep doing those, you are still operating at the same level and you are not growing and making sure you are really operating at the right level with your peers and the director and things like that. And I suppose that you can have confidence in the fact that I haven't read everything but I have thought about a couple of salient points that I want to raise here. So basically having confidence in the context of shorter time to prepare and be more efficient about how you operate yourself. So very helpful in that regard.

Kate takes the opportunity to *consider how she will collaborate* with her team of leaders. She uses the coaching to *consider what her 'ask' will be* from the team while also *calling on the team member expertise to gain collective insight* and *clarify expectations and performance levels* that she will *communicate to the team*.

> Secondly, to ask them what do they see that is good here, what do they think we could improve on and then give them an understanding of what I expect, because I have people here pretty much all at a manager level, so I don't have a huge mix of grade structures so there is a big expectation in terms of leadership and delivery from my perspective.

> So, the challenge now I would see is that people understand what is acceptable from my perspective and, also, I would think my deputy. She and I would be singing from the same hymn sheet in terms of a standard and particularly, given the level they are at, turnaround and adherence to deadlines, things like that, adding value. And also, what I would say is a real clear expectation that people take up ownership and responsibility for their work.

Kate was able to use resources provided by the coach to *develop her insight around interactions* she would have with others.

> . . . and just as a frame of reference so I would get articles from her as well and she would send me on things I could think about so just remind yourself in terms of your interactions.

Kate uses the coaching session to consider *interactions with her team members around performance conversations* and messaging while also *considering development opportunities* to *enable team member development*.

> I think it is important for your manager to point that out and I think as part of performance assessment in my view and we are in the middle of the process at this stage in terms of moderation. Like how I would always personally and I think others would rank others in terms of the exceptional category, where they do more than what is expected of them in terms of their job, because that is the contractual element.

> Doing the job well is not getting you into elevated performance categories. That is kind of your contract. And in terms of the scoring, we talked about this in terms of talent management. I think in some circumstances people don't understand that. They think that to be in the higher end of performance that it is OK to do your own job really well. Sometimes, that does not pan out that way because you have a peer group that you don't have visibility on and where we are comparing you against. And I suppose you have got to think how you differentiate yourself.

> I would say it is not enabling people to maximize that as well. It's a really important part of what we do: we kind of have to say this is what we want.

How is that going to happen for that person, maybe we have to throw other work their way. You have to enable people to have the chance to do that as well. So that is pretty important.

Kate reflects on how her *confidence level* can dip and realizes it is something that happens to others too. The *coach brings perspective* that *reminds Kate of her experience and capability*, which supports Kate as she makes the transition.

I suppose that you can have confidence in the fact that I haven't read everything but I have thought about a couple of salient points that I want to raise here so basically having confidence in the context of shorter time to prepare and be more efficient about how you operate yourself. So very helpful in that regard.

Some of the elements I would struggle with, would be you would have a bit of a crisis of confidence from time to time and I can be real candid about it and sometimes when you are in a new role and particularly when you come back from maternity leave. So, I think you can be very 'gung ho' when you are in an interview and you can be very good at selling yourself, but switch off that performance and you go and, particularly when you are on mat leave, and you come back a year later, you have got to remind yourself of those things.

Because she was very good at just reminding me of . . . so I do think it is probably something very sexist to say. I think it is something most women suffer from a lot, in terms of . . . so that's very beneficial in the context of just reminding me of little tools and techniques to remind yourself of what you know and your experience.

Kate *used feedback from the selection process* along with *insights from other feedback* she received regarding *her communications style*. This allows her to *reflect on her own development*

So, it's such an obvious question, what was your feedback at the last interview and what have you done subsequently and why don't you kind of structure that, and there was nothing in that feedback that I found that I disagreed with because it is a very good process. So, we had very good material, I think, to work with from that perspective.

Another piece of feedback I would have got as well is, in terms of my communication style, and this is something that I have been very conscious of is that not to be too elaborate in my communication and to be conscious of who my audience is. So more internally than externally, I think.

I have knocked it on the head because I have been dealing with external regulation for so many years, CEOs and things like that, but more internally in the context of being very conscious of the type of forum I am at, the type of committee structure and what is the point I want to make. That's me elaborating on what my feedback was. So that is what I am saying, I am learning from people.

Kate was starting to make that ***shift from being the content expert*** to where she now ***operates at the more strategic level***. She realizes that she needs to ***gain trust with her team*** and ***delegate work*** that she was previously competent in undertaking.

> Because you are the subject matter expert in all of that kind of stuff. Trusting your team, you know. So, I found her very, very helpful in the context of just kind of, as you become more senior in the organization, how you stop doing the things you had done before because otherwise if you keep doing those, you are still operating at the same level and you are not growing and making sure you are really operating at the right level.

Kate has some ***sustainable learning insights and tools*** she can carry forward with her as she ***works with her team***. Coaching has ***lifted her awareness*** and was ***developmental*** in terms of helping her ***adapt in her presence and effectiveness as a senior leader***. Coaching was also ***supportive in the earlier stage with promotional opportunity***. Kate continues to work on the ***behavioural changes*** and acknowledges that she will ***continue to learn*** as she moves forward.

> Yes, just some small tools made a significant difference in terms of, as I said, meeting preparation and things like that and I take copious notes when I am at these sessions and just as a frame of reference so I would get articles from her as well and she would send me on things I could think about so just remind yourself in terms of your interactions.

> It might have taken longer so I think she could have short circuited some of the issues I was grappling with myself so in a way that gave me tools that I wouldn't have been aware of.

> Well, in the first instance it has had the desired effect in terms of a promotional opportunity so I would like to think that I am behaving differently because I am taking some of the things that we are discussing. I think it's one of those things that you have to keep reminding yourself. I think that, like, one of my downfalls is I go to training sessions and I don't apply, like some people are very good and very disciplined about applying stuff afterwards and I find it really beneficial and I must remember that and I look back and my notes are fantastic and I am not . . . kind of.

> Yes, in certain circumstances I am applying stuff but I am still learning. It's not like I have got my feedback, I have been promoted and now I need to stop doing those things. I need to continue, continue, continue.

Kevin (No. 4)

Kevin has had 20 years' experience as a leader and his first experience of coaching was part of a leadership development programme, which was focused on building his leadership capability and helping him navigate change with his team. He has also become a coach within the organization. Kevin's latest role is

Head of Organizational Development for a large commercial body where he has ten direct reports.

The coaching was voluntary while the organization, which has a panel of external coaches, also encourages leaders to avail of coaching as they move into a new role. For this coaching intervention, there was no formal contracting with the coach or three-way meeting with his leader. Having selected a coach from the panel, they had a chemistry meeting and Kevin felt they were on the same wavelength and progressed with 6 × 1.5hr sessions over the following months.

While Kevin had 40 on his team in his last role and had 20 years' leadership experience, he realized the *transition piece* for him was not so much about the what but *more about the how to build a team to be the best that they could be.*

> When you got into the bigger organization, it's a bit of a more challenging thing.
>
> And myself, I was starting to realize that transition piece, even though I said I had been in a leadership role for 20 years, it was all about what you did rather than how you did it. You know, so I was getting more, much more interested in the how, yes, the how.

Kevin notes the main part of the coaching was around the questions being asked by the coach, which felt challenging and a *real reflection back to him*.

> In the middle of the thing, I think, is where most of the work was done where you are really being challenged, the questions that the coach was giving me were really challenging me.
>
> You know what I mean, the conversations, you know it's like looking in the mirror. You know it is, and they are doing it in such a way to get the best out of you, but sometimes it doesn't feel like that in the session.

The coach partnered with Kevin as he *reflected on an item he was dealing with* and where he could *look at all options* available to him. Through discussion he considered and *analysed all options* and *kept the options open longer* (without locking them down too early), which allowed more *critical thinking*.

> And I suppose the other really big thing is to think wider than you normally think. I think that . . . so you might think you have three options, but actually challenge yourself to say there are six to evaluate. Now, in some instances you don't have the time. You just might have to go. But I think the general thing is, it's a good thing to be reflective, sit back, think about it and then ultimately you have to make a decision, but it's really better if everyone is on the train.
>
> So, in all those sessions it was about laying out the options available and more importantly to keep all the options open. So, if you are there and you

are trying to transition to a new role and you have your heart set on X, but X isn't available, then what is Y and Z. And then we discussed those and the pros and cons of those and then maybe in three months' time, we will come back and see is that still the status or has something else come onto the table.

If coaching is anything, it needs to be a *psychologically safe place with trust and openness* for it to be really effective. There is no hierarchy in this partnership and he rationalized that the coach was not there to evaluate him so Kevin knew even if he felt somewhat vulnerable that he needed to be *open and honest* if he was to *get the most from the coaching.*

I suppose you know at the start there is that whole dynamic around the trust, you know, how open am I going to be with the coach. So, in other words, am I going to lay every single piece or am I going to stick to . . . the core issue is.

You know. So sometimes it's actually the stuff outside the core that is impacting on the core. You know if it is something to do with family, that's not necessarily related to work but if you can solve the family bit you can actually then have your mind clear or whatever. So, I think the first time I had the experience with the coach, there was a trust piece so it was late session 2 before I say, even though I knew I got on well with her at the chemistry check.

Because, at the end of the day, you know what I mean like, that trust piece, the coach is there. They are not there to question or evaluate you. They are there to sort of say . . . let's draw out a map here and let's look at the options, see which is the best for you at this moment in time.

While the coach is there to listen and ask questions for clarity, this helps Kevin to download and *unravel what is on his mind, gain clarity* that will help him *prioritize*. This relationship with the coach allows for an *honest conversation* that also considers more unconscious aspects too like *his values*.

I thought that was that bit that . . . so . . . I knew all those things myself, but they were all in a muddle. I thought the beauty of the coach was she was able to take them down, prioritize them, evaluate them with me and, at the end of the day, I was doing all the evaluation, but it was just the structure that was used, that was really helpful.

If I have a coaching intervention and I have a session with my coach, I can park all that baggage or all that concerns and just get on with the day job. So, I think that's a huge thing sometimes that people feel that an intervention whether it's a coach or a mentoring relationship, it allows you to get a really honest conversation and maybe clarify a few things around your own values and then park that or keep working on where you need to work on, being strategic and then come back and get on with the day job. Well that to me . . . that's our experience with a high IQ organization.

Kevin realizes, in his busy world, he needs to have time to **stretch his own thinking** as he reflects on **how he can be a great leader**. Feeling that push back from the coach helped him to **come up with his own insight, think broader and outside of the box, further than he would have done on his own**.

> It's trying to get the magic of the person coming up with the idea rather than you telling them. Yet you have to be pushy enough to get them to a point where they will think in a slightly different way, slightly outside the box. It broadens their thinking and it stretches it out.
>
> I think it opened my eyes to a wider lens. I think that's the real, real bit that . . . you know we are all here busy in the today, the now, whenever but really if we are going to be great leaders, we need to be out, further out here.
>
> You know what we are having in this whole performance management, this conversation which is the 'what' and the 'how'. So, you know I could have done a great 'what' and the team is dead at the end of the year. You know, whereas if I look after the 'how', then I will get the 'what' done. You can have a great year and have the team dead or you can have a great year and have the team energized to take it forward. It's long term and the lens was widened.

From time to time, a leader can find themselves in uncomfortable spaces and coaching allows a safe space to **express and understand emotions** and consider their **impact** and from there **self-manage**.

> and I think that's where the coach . . . because sometimes like that, you can sort of, you can let that be seen and you just need to be careful about . . . You do, because there is a long game here and the long game here is like the emotional intelligence. It is how can I hold myself in very uncomfortable spaces.

For Kevin, part of his transition was to **step back from the notion of his high level of expertise** and instead create **space for his managers and leaders to grow**.

> And also, myself to transition out of . . . I know the job more than the individuals that I have appointed, so how do I transition myself to give them their space to grow technically, but also to grow as people managers and leaders.

For leaders to get the most from people, it can be useful to have some **understanding or insight around personalities**. For Kevin, MBTI was his window that allowed some understanding, which helps him **navigate interactions and engagement with others**.

> Whereas it's a bit like the Myers Briggs, does it really hugely matter which of the 16 boxes you are in as long as you are aware of it and what it means when you are interacting with someone else. And you know you are here as

an extravert and someone else is here as an introvert, somehow you both have to move a little bit but if you are over there and they are over there, there is always going to be tension. So, it is helpful to navigate those journeys.

And I suppose in that Myers Briggs it's strange. I am an extravert, my boss is an introvert and even managing that relationship is energy, whereas I am anxious to move and my boss is, yes, but we will have to replace you and the coach even trying to manage that relationship when it's an extravert vs an introvert.

During coaching, Kevin reflected on how he could *bring the team with him* and *consider how he might engage with team members* and after those meetings, review with the coach and then consider *what he might need to do beyond that* to ensure all were with him, as he navigated his way forward.

And really the coaching was around navigating that journey as I interacted with the team, trying to sell to high IQ people that their emotions are important and raising that with the team and going back to the coach with How will I approach it? These guys are busy, these girls are busy, you know and that was really it. Trying to go on the journey . . . it's navigating it, you know what I mean. So erm . . . that was the first experience with the coaching.

It was a good team. It wasn't that I was doing it because the team was poor, I wanted to make a very good team great, so that is where we were starting from and they were happy to go on the journey. So that was really the bit, it was really touching in around that.

So, I think that is one of the big things that I think you know I might have an ambition to take the team, but unless I keep them fully informed all the way through the process, then they won't stay with you. Now, in some instances, you know, not everyone on the team needs to be told every bit of detail or whatever.

During coaching, Kevin *reflected on performance conversations* and with particular focus on the 'how' and the 'what' of performance as it was important for Kevin as a leader to *keep the team energized* and he understood he could influence the sustaining of that energy. Equally, he reflected on times when he held more difficult conversations around people's performance. Leaders need to be able to have those performance conversations and coaching provided Kevin a reflective space to consider those conversations with his team.

You know what we are having in this whole performance management, this conversation which is the 'what' and the 'how'. So, you know I could have done a great 'what' and the team is dead at the end of the year. You know whereas if I look after the 'how', then I will get the 'what' done. You can have a great year and have the team dead or you can have a great year and have the team energized to take it forward.

Think that's the thing as well having done the coaching. Now some of those conversations may be less adult to adult, (laugh) because the truth . . . I think you need to let people know that on an ongoing basis. So even the training or the opportunities for training or if someone is struggling, I am not sending them off on training and they are struggling to get their job done.

So, you would try and explain some of those and you need to get back on track. But in a general sense it is rare that I find I ever went to the extreme of saying to someone I think you should leave this company. But that would be very unusual. No one wanted to work with the individual. They did leave.

A light bulb moment came for Kevin through the challenges, questioning and probing from coaching in the past when Kevin came to **understand what leadership means for him** and, as he says, it is the **mark he wants to leave as a leader**. Leaders can **grow other leaders** through empowering and allowing others to have autonomy in their work and Kevin wants to **grow successful leaders** on the back of his own leadership. Coaching has created some momentum for Kevin as he has made his leadership journey.

And myself, I was starting to realize that transition piece, even though I said I had been in a leadership role for 20 years, it was all about what you did rather than how you did it. You know, so I was getting more, much more interested in the how, yes, the how.

I said the word light bulb. It totally changed. The light bulb moment for me was the first time I worked with a coach, because it was the first time that I saw that difference between managing and leading. Up to that, even though I had classroom interventions or whatever, but some of those trainings are really text bookie, but through the challenges and the questions and the probings of the coach, it was the first time I really got that click.

Yeah, I now really appreciate even though I had done leadership in college but I think it was really that opportunity to say this is about you now and what mark do you want to leave as a leader whereas up to that . . . this is what leadership is generally about and take it or leave it.

She introduced me to a book by Goffee and Jones 'Why Should Anybody Be Led By You' and that to me was a light bulb moment.

If I never read another book about leadership that was sort of one of the things I took away from it. Absolutely, no one is not talent today. The question is what is their appetite and ambition. But also, a little bit of a lift up . . . if you can raise everybody up and others grow on the back of others. It causes a momentum or like a snowball going down the hill and it suddenly becomes massive.

In between coaching sessions, Kevin undertook a *short 360-degree feedback survey* along with his team and the feedback guided a way forward that was *useful for some personal stretch and growth*.

> We had this whole thing about leadership is something you do with people rather than to people. And then sort of looked at the profile of the team and also looked at my profile, which is where we looked and myself as leader and to see where I am strong, what I am weak in, what would I start, stop and continue. That type of thing. Did a 360 with the team . . . only those three questions really . . . there weren't 50 questions.

> The following coaching sessions focused on re-affirming the good, so not to lose those and mostly about the stops. I suppose the rest of the coaching was about how we can grow.

John (No. 5)

John has six years' experience as a leader and is very developmentally focused and has strongly invested in furthering his personal and professional development. He is a continuous learner and holds a diverse range of qualifications that all support his technical expertise.

As he took on his latest leadership role leading a team of 30 people within the area of market trading regulation, he has sought an external coach who has worked with people who were making transitions. He wanted to work on the transition across to a new senior leadership role, in terms of managing himself and in order to plan a progressive course across the line to ensure he managed the transition well.

Leaders who are unfamiliar with coaching have their own ideas of what coaching offers. So it is important that the coach does not assume prior knowledge and checks in with the client. Depending on the client's experience of working with a coach, the coach can decide on the level of detail they need to provide around what coaching is and is not. This is where contracting comes to the fore along with professional ethics and boundaries. For John in the early years, he thought the coach was more of a guide and has since *learned what coaching offers*.

> I didn't really have a great idea about what coaching was or I had my idea that they would come to me . . . like they would be doing the talking and I would be doing the listening. So that is basically where it started.

> Again, it's yes . . . and in the interim I have done the Coaching Diploma and I coach people internally and externally. So now I have much more of an idea of what coaching is and the potential benefits of it.

> From the first session I was much clearer about what I wanted to get out of it and much clearer in terms of are we off on the right path and much clearer. But these are self-identified areas. I met the coach and I booked my next session. I think someone else telling you (your manager) what you need to

work on is just that piece of information but if I don't see it myself. I think the 360 is useful but if I don't see that myself, my commitment to working on it is over.

Coaching can be a *support to the leader* when they find themselves in what can be an isolating place when they are *not familiar with the new terri-tory* and need a thinking partner who can work with them as they navigate their way

> But now I was moving to a new division with different functional areas linked to market so the markets experience was useful, but that wasn't necessarily what I was working on, so I needed to . . .

> I suppose I am making a transition and it's a transition both from where I worked in financial markets and risk under X Company. I never worked in financial regulation. I was making a transition across to a totally different division but basically no one would really know me and so I felt in that context that really what I could do with is something that could help me.

The coaching environment creates a *different dynamic* that can be very help-ful for the leader.

> You can underestimate that when you leave the office and you go to a differ-ent place and you talk about yourself and you're listened to and that sort of environment . . . that's good in a way.

John's *awareness has been heightened* through having his assumptions challenged and he can see the *impact of those assumptions* and their *link to his behaviour* that was limiting him.

> I think what the coaching addressed was the way I view myself and the assumptions I was making about myself, how these assumptions were man-ifesting themselves in behaviour and how these behaviours were limiting my ability to progress in my impact or whatever, so not life and death issues but there still were, shall we say, the little nagging issues that interrupt your flow in terms of work so it was good to be able to come to a place and hear those issues in a way and maybe have my assumptions challenged around them and then be pushed towards solutions rather than sort of focusing on the issues themselves and to get different perspectives. So, I found that part very useful.

For the leader to be able to *safely share and express what is happening* for them and then to *reach some clarity* is so often how coaches support their client.

> Because I wasn't quite clear on certain things and so she did facilitate on things that I didn't know . . . I found it useful but I guess I would have found

it more useful if I was really clear about what I wanted to work on. I found it a big support in terms of being able to sort of go to a room and air what was going on with me.

And the safe space that coaching provides where the leader can *speak their truth* without judgement is very valuable.

and just in that kind of space like in that environment where you could basically say whatever you wanted. That was the most useful part of it.

John specifically chose to work with a coach who worked with leaders in transition. This provided that safe and supportive space for John to *identify key items* and *make a plan* with a number of items *both tangible and intangible*. From there he would *look at his options*, *take steps* and review them over the course of the coaching sessions. Even high achieving and very competent leaders can *push out their own performance level* and John saw that transitioning was that opportunity for *further stretch*, even if it was for *that extra 5 per cent*.

I was making a transition across to a totally different division but basically no one would really know me and so I felt in that context that really what I could do with is something that could help me tap into my own sort of resources and help me to sort of look at things from a different perspective. What I was really looking towards in the profiles was someone that worked with people who were making transitions.

So, I was conscious that somebody that would be able to help me to work on that transition across both in terms of managing myself and then, you know, having a sort of planned progressive transition across the line, that I was managing that transition well, if you know what I mean. I was anxious to sort of, well I suppose it is like anything, if there is an extra 5 per cent in it, you should go for it, for that extra 5 per cent. But I felt that was the right decision to make.

Part of the transition to a senior leadership role will be the impact and influence with various stakeholders across the organization and *especially with their peers in the senior leadership forum*. Here feedback can be helpful for the leader as they *gain that confidence* and understand what they might *stop doing* or *start doing*, so *adjustments in behaviour* that is likely to *have more impact*.

The other thing that she talked about, which I thought was very good. She caught me being longwinded and then she stopped me and she said 'now this is what I am hearing, is that your intention' and it was just those sorts of impact and influence pieces, being able to reframe. So, to hear how she was experiencing me was very useful as well.

My current coaching arrangement is around the transition and the impact I will have in my new directorate.

My impact and influence particularly with senior management because at times I may talk around things and I give more of a context than what is needed. I may not be as direct or point focused or, you know . . . there are three things here, the first is this . . . the second is this and the third is this . . . I don't always approach things in that way.

I would give more context than what I need to. I may be over staff-focused, but the main thing is the impact and influence on senior managers, being able to articulate myself in short bursts and land the message that needs to be landed, but do that sort of in a concise way.

Anytime a person is making a change, the opportunity to check in with someone **holds the person accountable to themself** and coaching **offers that discipline and support**.

I found the check in and actually where I would say 'this is what I have done'. There was a certain discipline around all of that that was obviously useful.

. . . and then the follow-up and what have you done since the last time. What worked and what didn't work and just in that kind of space like in that environment where you could basically say whatever you wanted. That was the most useful part of it.

Coaching provided opportunities through conversations for John to open up to **new possibilities** that he was unlikely to reach on his own. He can tap into his **inner strengths and values and ways of knowing**. The coach can be the mirror and reflect back to the client both any strengths or blind spots. This reflection and feedback by the coach can bring about **new awareness** for the leader that can be significantly developmental.

Facilitating the opening up of possibilities that are your possibilities but you are very unlikely to tap into them or see them yourself. That is what I would see . . . and it is like anything, when someone does something very well, like this lady has done in my own coaching and I think 'Do I do that?' Could I open up those possibilities with that?

It's that sort of tapping into your own resources you don't even know you have and those resources creating the possibilities for different things, different areas of development that you didn't necessarily think were there. You weren't aware of, I suppose. It's transformative and it is exciting, for me that is what the a . . . and because you identify them yourself, because they are your possibilities, you sort of go at them that little bit harder than if somebody else suggested them to you.

During the coaching, the leader undertook an ECR (Emotional Capital Report) assessment and this provided **feedback on leadership potential**, which he found very useful. **Self-awareness** allows the leader to identify a measure of their emotional intelligence. From there the leader can take steps to achieve any desired change. Again, progress towards any change identified can be discussed and reviewed at coaching sessions.

> To a degree you could say the psychometrics; the ECR helped a bit with that in terms of my confidence, my straightforwardness. These are the areas that are more confidence related, if we want to call them that. It certainly helped me identify them but also gave me hope that there was a way to improve if I took certain actions or if I . . . . self-identified actions that these are things that I could work on and improve. That is really what I got that was very useful out of it.

The more aware and comfortable a leader is in their own role and where they can trust themselves, then the more they can start to **trust their team** and **develop the team**, which is not a threat to them. On reflection now, John has seen that and **identified a particular strength** he has, which is **identifying and developing leadership talent**, a very valuable competence to have as a leader in today's world.

> I am reasonably relaxed with myself so because of that then I am quite comfortable then sharing my strengths but also my development points with people around me and being open and just establishing that level of trust, basically to be able to develop good teams, to develop good leaders too. One way I would call myself is like a multiplier so that I can develop good teams and develop good people.

Through this transitional coaching, the coach facilitated a gestalt exercise using figures or objects to represent people in the organization and John was able to experiment with placing them and himself within the system, which all gave him a high-level overview of the wider system which also created new insights for him.

This approach **opened up opportunities and possibilities** for the leader, which he described as **light bulb moments**. John found the way it was undertaken and with the questions that followed very powerful and **more emerged** while the effects of **waking up his thinking** were still there for some hours later.

> The last coaching session we had, I mean, I do coaching internally now but what she did, she got me into a sort of a . . . using figures and bits of things and asking where are you and where is everybody else and where do you want them to be? You know it was sort of very conceptual but it was very . . . I found it was huge, it brought up so many different opportunities or possibilities and I think that is the value of it.

> It wasn't that the possibilities came from her. It was facilitated by her but it came from me. That is what the value was. I actually walked in from a location after it, which is about 8 kilometers or something like that, and I felt great after it. I felt I needed the walk just to think out all these things,

these opportunities and possibilities that were going through my head, following it.

Certainly, the way this was done, more emerged perhaps rather than from a conversation because it is different . . . it was just those kind of questions, where are you in relation to this group and it is natural in terms of . . . but if someone had said to me think about this. It was just . . . I wouldn't have been able to match that.

When John was asked if there were times or stages when the coaching had more impact he noted:

Well, I think there are two major insights with the last coaching session. So the first was around that piece and using the spaces and just that different piece and the way she did it was . . . it generated more insights than a . . . and I found it particularly useful there. The other thing that she talked about which I thought was very good. She caught me being longwinded and then she stopped me and she said 'now this is what I am hearing, is that your intention' and it was just those sort of impact and influence pieces, being able to reframe. So to hear how she was experiencing me was very useful as well. So they are the two major pieces from that specific coaching session.

Paul (No. 6)

Paul has 20 years' experience in leadership roles across different functions within the same organization. His most recent role is director with a global remit for supply chain management in an organization of 13,000 employees globally. He has six direct reports and separately he is leading a temporary project team, which has 40 team members.

HR scheduled all newly appointed senior executives onto a global senior leadership development programme where coaching is also an integral part of the 12-month programme. Paul met with an external coach for eight sessions during that time. At the start, there was a tripartite meeting with Paul's leader and another meeting at the end. The last session was around the transition from working with the coach to working with his leader going forward.

Even though Paul held previous leadership roles, he acknowledges it is still new territory and is a significant step change to director level. He was *getting to grips with the new role, accountabilities* and all the aspects he needs to pay attention to from different angles as he *makes the necessary adjustments* to his new role.

It was all quite new territory for me in terms of a new role and moving into a director position and those accountabilities and there was a lot going on in the day job as you can imagine with all of that.

I suppose getting to grips with a new role at quite a senior level and the accountabilities and dealing with all the adjustment to that. So, I had been a line manager before. So it wasn't new, but this was on a bigger scale and more senior people reporting into me. And I had been on leadership teams before but now I was on more senior leadership teams in this role, so all that adjustment there and dealing with some new processes, systems, getting up to speed, learning about stuff that I needed to learn about, quickly building a lot of relationships, you know vertically, horizontally.

Paul wanted a stronger challenge and *requested that the coach be more challenging*. He felt he would have got more value from a more challenging style of engagement and discussed it with the coach. Yet he still felt he *could have been challenged more by the coach*.

As personal style and culture will be part of the dynamic that the coach is working within, a question for a coach is, how will I know if I am supporting or challenging the client enough and how comfortable am I in adapting my approach, if required? Also, could I be supporting the client too much when I should be challenging them more or vice versa?

Yes, the coaching was good. On hindsight and I reflected on this, probably half way through the coaching, I mean I am so busy, Did I really realize the value of that opportunity because, I mean, that was a huge investment from the organization and from the business of my time. I mean, just financially the total cost of that would have been very significant for each individual.

And I was conscious of that and took it seriously, but did I really extract as much value as I could have from it? I am not sure I did. I certainly could have for the first half and then I sort of did stop and think and I did say to my coach that I felt it was too safe, it was too punctual and I said that to her. And I asked her and my request was for her to be more provocative, more challenging, don't give me an easy ride, because I said 'I don't think it is your fault because I am probably maybe participating in this conversation probably in a way that is 80 per cent of what it should be from my perspective'.

More of a challenge, yes and earlier on, but because I was so busy spinning so many plates, it wasn't . . . a . . . but in hindsight I do have a few regrets and if I was coaching somebody about it, I would say be really . . . and I did coaching with some other folks and I would be really clear up front, this is a fantastic opportunity, so almost over-emphasize in your own mind what you want to get out of it, so I think my coach who in ways was fantastic, because her style was very engaging. I mean other people, I know their coaches practically thumped them, you know it was like in a psychological sense, but really kind of shook them and I know some folks really appreciated that and felt, wow, it was great. They really grabbed me by the ankles and turned me upside down and really put me through the wringer.

My coach would never ever do that. And even when I made a challenge around the provocation bit, she did shift the emphasis but still . . . in a way it probably let me off the hook a bit in that 'did she really cause me to challenge me' as much as I could have and should have.

She probably didn't. I have to take some of the blame for that because they . . . it's like any counsellor or coach, it's not about . . . you know you are helping the person to figure it out themselves ultimately, the coach does not have to figure it out for them. So, I don't expect her to figure it all out for me. But could she have at an earlier stage said to me, 'Paul I think you are treading water a bit here, are you really grabbing this and wrestling with some of the issues?' So, in ways, I got an awful lot from the conversation over the year.

Paul as a leader is focused on **understanding what the future needs are** as much as well as **what is needed presently**, all of which will bring balance and influence the **right things to be busy with**.

For me, there is something around, to distil it down, it is that sense of being busy at the right things and therefore to do that, you have got to stand in the future. You have got to take that longer-term view. If you stand too long in the future, you stand the risk of the day to day, you lose that focus of today, tomorrow, next week so you end up almost naval gazing so there is a balance to be had there.

Paul uses his critical thinking to **consider the challenges and opportunities of the future** and to **find better ways** to get ready and be **set up for the future**. Here again, Paul **notes a lack of challenge from the coach to stretch his thinking**. Holding him accountable would also have been a part of the benefit of this challenge.

So I suppose I always have had a restlessness and an interest in looking beyond the status quo and thinking OK, so what should we be doing or thinking about differently in the context of being better set up for the future and being better able to operate to deal with the challenges and opportunities that arise, etc. So that is what I like to do, so when I work myself or when I am doing a bit of work with others.

On reflection afterwards, I sort of felt 'Do you know what if I was her, I would have been more challenging'. I would have said 'Hold on Paul, based on our previous conversation a month ago, whenever, I am not sure you are really addressing the issue or the opportunity or the challenge. I think you are . . .' So, probably, in that sense, she could have caused me to be more challenging of myself in terms of some of the opportunities, some of the risks I maybe perceived. And I think I probably left something behind in that process. I am not hung up on it because overall it was a great process.

For Paul, clarity and focus and success ultimately is about **being busy at the right things**.

Because people can ask me and pull me into this piece of work and that piece of work and a bit of strategy work there and I like it. I am interested in it and you could spend your whole day doing it. The thing is, I have other staff and I need to focus on their . . . they are probably the two main areas, but there are others.

But oftentimes, in my head, I have a belief that lots of companies have failed or relationships have failed. It's not because people set out to fail, but they are often busy at the wrong things. And what I like to try and do is say how can we be busy at the right things.

During the coaching process, *feedback and lifting self-awareness* plays a part in the personal change that needs to be supported. Here Paul realizes he needs to *stretch his relationships and networks further*.

If I am really being serious about my purpose, it's taking my networks further in terms of my relationships further, so I do it but I am probably too conservative about how hard I push that. My feedback recently from my line manager to a greater degree is . . . ? I will do it in relation to the networks I am comfortable in. Beyond that I am more . . . I don't not do it but I am more cautious with how I do it and the provocation is to do that more and to a higher degree.

Even at the most senior levels, the leader *can experience a dip in confidence* as they move into a new role. Doubts can creep in and this is where CBC can be helpful as a tool to understand and challenge those doubts. While the leader can feel somewhat vulnerable, hopefully through the supportive relationship with a coach, the leader can fully be themselves and feel safe enough to express those thoughts.

Again, this can be something that is hidden and a mindful coach can look out for any dip in confidence. This was an interesting paradox with Paul, in so far, that he would have liked more of a challenge overall from his coach and yet he was experiencing doubts around his ability to take on the role. A coach may never know the deeper psychological work they are touching on when they engage with a client and again that is where their own supervision is a critical element of their own development.

You have got to get your own head around your own confidence levels in your role, like that, and I think just feeling ready and able for the role. And for me as I have experience in my role of coaching other people, you know with the sound of the voice in your head, 'can you really, are you really able for this, can you really do it?' And dealing with that voice in your head was part of it. So, all of those things.

Overall, the coaching facilitated Paul as he *explored his purpose, leadership possibility, future focus and looked at legacy* over the next few years. In general, he feels that part worked well. So while Paul felt the *coach could have been more challenging*, there were *aspects that worked well*.

I would be better positioned to do what I needed to do as a leader and I was quite open to the whole purpose bit. You know, some people maybe struggled a bit with that . . . it's kind of getting into my private life, my work life balance and values and my private life. Now, in fairness to them, they were not trying to act as clinical psychologists. I mean, it wasn't like the psychologist's chair or anything like that but some people might have felt . . . like I was quite open to all that exploration about purpose and meaning.

I wasn't over burdened with expectation other than I expected it to be positive, I expected it to help me to explore purpose and meaning and my leadership possibility in the context of my new role, I expected to do that and I expected the unexpected. I wasn't overburdened about pre-conceptions of what it would and wouldn't do.

It did help me crystallize a view of my purpose in its broadest sense of work and life, which is great, and it did help me to explore my leadership possibility and I liked the future focus bit so it was that whole notion of your legacy as you look out three or four years' time and I did all of that very well. I thought that worked well.

Marion (No. 7)

Marion has been in leadership roles for the past four years. Her new role as senior leader has a global remit. As Head of Function for a supply chain for a large global company within the Information technology industry, she has an overall team of 75 people across nine countries. Marion decided she wanted to work with an external coach as she navigated the first 90 days. She engaged in six sessions over 12 months. A key focus for her was gaining techniques to coach and develop her overall team, which was dispersed over nine geographical sites. This role was a significant step change for Marion and she wanted to work on building up her confidence also as she stepped up into this more senior executive role.

The *discipline of creating space* and reflection with the support of questions helped Marion *get a reality check* on her own thoughts.

I think you have to be more disciplined and I think it's funny because we did discuss this the last day and she talked about the fact that she does some self-coaching herself and she shared with me her coaching questions and it is really about me having the discipline for me to book myself into this room and do a coaching session for myself. But I think that probably is quite hard but I think doing it with colleagues . . . I think I can do it with people that I trust.

Moving to more senior leadership role calls for a more strategic approach where a vision for the future can be shaped. Marion knows that *creating the future picture* is not the most natural for her, so she will need some support as she *develops a strategic vision*.

I always say give me something and tell me what you want me to get to . . . you and I have no problem getting all the people together to get us there, but actually coming up with where there is, is a bit more challenging. So, the longer-term strategic vision of it.

Other sessions I might have looked at were my strategy, my vision for the cluster and things like that.

I think one of my sort of biggest challenges is coming with the big ideas so a bit more challenge around the creativity or the innovation.

Through questioning from the coach Marion was able to widen her lens with **critical thinking** and in that space she gained **clarity, visibility and results**.

I think it just gave me the space to be able to explore sometimes things that were not that big of a challenge until you discussed them and put them out on the table and then you think they are a challenge. It gave me the space to work through things. It gave me clarity, visibility and results. All of which coaching is all about. You do it all yourself. It's just someone sitting across from you asking all the right questions you know which is pretty powerful.

Marion acknowledges that coaching offers the **safe place** where she can be **totally open** and **express any fears or concerns**. Coaching is that place with no hierarchy or judgement.

For me, my view always on these things is unless you give them everything pretty much, they are not going to be able to coach you very well.

At the front end, I feel it was very much like a safety blanket or something and it was just a really safe space to come into, a place to bounce ideas around and to get feedback.

I think for me the coaching is really about having a really safe environment where you can open up about what your fears or concerns are or what are the challenges you are facing or things that you might have to encounter.

I think it brought me, I suppose, nearly like a sense of comfort, a sense of clarity and just really a safe environment to work through the challenges that I was facing.

Through coaching conversations and some reflection, the leader can **gain a broader perspective** by developing a wider lens.

I think I have figured a lot out over the year anyway while working with her and about, you know, certain things and seeing individuals, for example, my boss in different lights and realizing that there are different views, different opinions. It is not always one is right and one is wrong.

The impact a new leader makes on their team is important and while in coaching Marion **crafted her story**, which she would deliver to her team across the globe. She acknowledged that coaching helped her **achieve a level of focus** that she may not have achieved on her own.

One of the things I needed to do was to have a story to tell them. So one of the sessions was focused on crafting my leadership story and what was it and really helping me to get to the nuts and bolts of it and my big driver was it needed to be authentic.

Definitely when I was crafting the leadership story. That was probably the highlight, that I came out with a story that I was so happy with and went around and told nine different markets at that stage. Erm . . . I would have come up with a version of it, but I don't think it would have been as strong. I don't think it would have been as focused and I just think it wouldn't have been as impactful.

And then another one of the sessions focused very much on us having . . . I was having a big workshop with all the heads of the markets together and about prepping for that and the sort of stuff that I wanted to do at that session and getting some teamwork and just prepping and getting ideas how to run that session.

Marion found *mapping things out* on a flip chart helped *shape things* and also helpful to *develop a plan*.

In the middle then it was more so actually planning 'and this is what I am planning and helping me shape things'. You know. One of the comments my coach would have given me is that she feels it is quite easy coaching me because I am quite open to it and I sort of know what I want to do anyway. Sometimes it is probably literally that assurance and somebody to talk it out loud with and map it out. We stood in this room many times with a flip chart and mapped things out.

The coach is that *sounding board* as the leader *navigates* their way.

So, at the beginning it was very much a sounding board and a check in place and a finding my way.

If coaching is being done really well they shouldn't be giving you a huge amount. They should just be leading you and helping you get to where you can get to and yeah dropping in a few ideas along the way.

Results in organizations are not only achieved by leaders but through the engagement of their team and their achievements. Marion recognizes one of her strengths is a *focus on people and those relationships* as much as she is driven to achieve results.

So, for me, it is all about relationships with people, to know the people, to recognize the good work and rewarding them. The results will then take care of themselves afterwards I feel and that has always worked for me.

I feel very, very, results focused and driven to deliver really, really, high results but it is not my No. 1 priority and I suppose some of the technical aspects of the job sort of bored me a little bit, you know. Doing the stuff with the people is where I get excited.

A leader's confidence can take a dip as they take on a more senior role and Marion acknowledges that as she *opened up* to the coaching conversations, she is now more open to having similar conversations with other people she trusts as she moves forward. Also during this time, she has *built up more self-belief*, which was a big piece for her.

> I think probably one of the things I realized after doing it for the last eight months, I can probably do a lot more of that now with people that I trust well in here and maybe that is part of the confidence piece that has been built over the period.
>
> But I think a big piece was, one of my biggest challenges that I wanted to address was I suppose building up my own belief in myself and maybe seeing myself as others seem to see me as there may be a bit of a mismatch between those two. So that was a big part of it, building up my confidence, I suppose, in taking on the role.
>
> And that came out of one of the coaching sessions that actually what I do is that I figure out what the right thing to do is and that is what I do and my right thing to do is somebody else's as well. So I sort of hold on to that and not get too panicked about these big . . .
>
> I think I can do it with people that I trust. You know, recently, somebody asked me for a session to go through their career plan, a peer of mine, and then I asked her to return the favour and to have a discussion around a challenge I was having.

In terms of development tools, Marion used the coaching opportunity to *review her strengths* from a report she had already received recently and prior to coaching.

> I had done the strength deployment inventory in a previous course just recently and I brought that in and we reviewed that.

Richard (No. 8)

Richard has five years leadership experience and his more recent appointment is to a senior leader role where he has four direct reports and 29 people on the wider team. He was working for one of the 'Big Four' consultancy firms before taking on his current role. He has a strong developmental background having undertaken extensive studies and learning. This was his first experience of working with a coach and his initial perception of coaching prior to commencing work with a coach was very different from what he experienced (in a very positive way). He requested to work with an external coach focusing on his personal development in the area of emotional intelligence and he also wanted to carve steps further in his career to a more senior level (director). He undertook 8 × 1.5hr coaching sessions over eight months.

Depending on the leader's previous experience of working with a coach, the client can have **preconceived ideas of what coaching is** and Richard perceived that the coach would advise him on tactics for the senior executive role. When the coach started with questions and a deeper enquiry, Richard felt **a little unnerved** and it took a short while for him to **open to the questions and probing** and to see them in a positive light. This could be the first time that the leader has experienced this type of engagement.

> Initially it was . . . I won't say unnerving but it was a bit outside of my comfort zone. I didn't know this person and we started to get into quite personal conversations. So, it took me a while to feel at ease and I am not used to being challenged to the extent that this lady challenged me as well.
>
> And to be asked and the question kept coming back: Why? Why? Why do you want this? Why do you want that and I suppose, to be honest, I would have been arrogant would be a wrong word but I would have got a senior enough position quite young, so I had been thinking I am doing very well and erm . . . this person quite categorically put me in the box and said it is not really about the age that you are, but when you have this opportunity to progress, seize it because you may not get that opportunity or clear run of luck or whatever in different periods of your life. So, I suppose that is the specifics but I was kind of interested in those push backs and challenge, so I found the whole thing quite challenging. Yes, challenging is the right word but in a good way.

Richard **got frustrated** when the **most visible solution to a problem wouldn't work** in his organization. Coaching questions and probing can allow clarity to emerge but coaching is not a magic bullet the client may be looking for. Sitting with the client's emotion is a part of the coach's own journey. How might this impact the coach and the coaching relationship? If it impacts the coach, this may be something that the coach can bring to supervision?

> So they would ask, they would probe and maybe they kind of helped clear my thoughts but I had come very clearly to the answer so I would own the answer but then I would go with, well, that clearly won't work, no, no, no and that's where it got a bit messy. Does that make sense to you?
>
> I did have, I think, a kind of a challenge where I would come back to the (coach) and say I think that is the ultimate solution but that solution isn't right for where I am working and she didn't always agree with me on that and I kind of started to kind of [pause] challenge her credibility on some of her recommendations because what you are saying is fine but it just cannot be done in an organization like ours or another public sector organization or whatever.
>
> And the more I am in this organization since, the more it reinforces that idea that there is curtailment there to some of the quick things we can do or not.

I think the issue I had was I was developing myself but I still wasn't able to implement or gain traction or results to the space that I needed to get to. So that is probably less the coach's issue. But I think the coach could probably have a better understanding of what it is like to be in this sector. They came from banking and it's different.

Coaching can be that space where the leader can *reflect on issues* and *consider options*.

The middle part of it was about kind of problem-solving, problem-solving big bottleneck blocker issues that are stopping me getting the way of where I need to get to for the business.

During coaching, Richard got *clarity and focus* and from here he *identified key priorities*. Richard also got *insight around his own limits* and the *impact of taking on too much change*.

And the other one which is very important is focussing on the knitting, getting the three to five things and focus on them and get rid of the noise.

But it gave me a real understanding that there is only so much big change you should take on at any one time in order for you to do it properly, in order for you to flourish. So, it is one thing I am very cognizant of in my work and my home life, only a certain amount of things are taken on at any one time because it was way too much. And I got that . . . [pause] I wouldn't have . . . I didn't get that clarity elsewhere.

Over the coaching sessions, Richard worked through *real-life case studies at work*, *reviewed them* with his coach and *planned the next move forward*.

I would bring specific real-life examples of issues I was having at work and we would tease them out as a case study and in the following three or four or even five weeks I would look at dealing with that issue before I would go back to her so that I would have something to look at and look forward to as well.

Over time, Richard *shifted from being the expert* and started to *delegate more*. He started to take a *more strategic approach* and could now see where he could *add more value*.

So, I delegate like hell and I challenge what I should and shouldn't be part of and what I add value to and you can get recognition for and all these sorts of things. So, one learning is what you do.

I became less detail centric. I became more overview, strategic. I delegated a bit more but as a consequence of this I found myself less busy because I would have always been the one previously to get down to the detail and

> make sure that I knew as much as everyone else and I do well to fill up eight hours now.

> But I am even less busy than I was before but I do think I can add more strategic value add.

Richard found some of the **learning he took from the coaching** had an impact when he was handling some **tricky HR issues** at work.

> They [coach] had more impact for me when I was dealing with personnel issues. The more and more I have been involved in leadership roles, the more I have understood that the work itself is not rocket science. It's dealing with the people that can be the tricky one. Some of the most mundane small little things would come up and become huge issues and I became a lot more resolute in terms of determining what the right thing was and doing it in a kind of an appropriate manner and sticking by my guns and I dealt with some very tricky HR issues using some of the coaching learnings I had as kind of fuel to get to where I needed to get to.

Coaching conversations can touch on the **unconscious drives and motivations** and Richard appreciated **tapping into that personal insight**. He was already a very high achiever and very capable but he still **appreciated the reassurance** from the coach that he was capable of taking on this role. This also shows that **confidence levels** can take a dip at time of transition regardless of perceived readiness.

> She never actually asked what I do day to day but just wanted to get an understanding of my motivations, where I see myself going, how I feel about myself in terms of what drives me. All those sorts of things, the inner workings, the subconscious and I found that to be excellent and a bit unnerving initially. It was excellent and I suppose it was a bit like a tap, once it got turned on, it flew out of me and it gave me a deeper appreciation of what is important. So not necessarily being the smartest in the room or not knowing the most in the room but how to channel all these things together. So, I found it very useful.

> Sorry, I definitely reinforced my beliefs that it wasn't just me that thought I could do these things. This lady is an executive coach talking to me, saying yeah you are well able for these things as well and that kind of reinforced that piece.

Through the coaching Richard found a way to **understand** and consider how **best he could be** with **his own authentic leadership style**.

> Her main piece was you will get to where you want to get to by getting the most out of yourself or your style and if you try and tailor it and it is nearly like putting a harness on a horse or something, they are not going to be what they could be.

> So, it is about being authentic. So, you really have to flourish for what you are rather than fit yourself into a box. Which senior leaders if you meet them in organizations, they spend their time telling you to get into a box. That's why I find sometimes that she was totally different.

Leaders may also start considering their next career move, even as they move into their current new role. Coaches can often be a safe space with objectivity to leaders who are looking to the future at the *next career move*.

> I had been brought onto the senior leadership group in this company and I think I may have been considered before but I kind of reined in my brashness a bit and I think I wouldn't have got that opportunity if I had been as brash as I originally had been. So yeah, it probably wouldn't have happened but it was a result of it [the coaching].

> On that point one thing I think is very important and it is that it's the difference between someone who thinks they are helping you in your career but isn't doing you much good (internally) and this sort of coaching.

6 Leadership Transition Coaching Framework

The *Leadership Transition Coaching Framework is* made up of four main themes and a number of subordinate themes. The themes relate to the impact of coaching on the leaders as they worked with a coach while transitioning into a new role. While these results are applicable to all the leaders, it is worth noting they exist on a continuum and are supported by illustrative examples from the individual leaders.

- Time to think
- Clarity and focus
- Collaborate with others
- Development

The overall findings extensively cover all key aspects that were found through interviews with the eight leaders.

Theme 1 – time to think

Subordinate themes:

- Finding your feet in a new dynamic
- Discipline of reflecting to create value in a very busy world
- Have thinking and assumptions challenged
- Create space to think and plan to develop vision and direction
- Widen the lens with critical thinking to explore challenges and opportunities.

Theme 2 – clarity and focus

Subordinate themes:

- A psychologically safe environment with trust and openness
- Download and get structure on the issues
- Broaden perspective by developing a wider lens
- Operate at the right level for impact and influence
- Gain clarity and focus on priorities and develop a plan
- Check-in to review and revise
- Working smart and sustaining focus and energy.

Theme 3 – collaborate with others

Subordinate themes:

- Collaborate with new leadership team (leader of leaders) to develop one vision
- Flex approach for effective interactions and engagement with different personalities
- Navigate the journey with the team and bring them onboard
- Setting expectations and performance conversations
- Build new relationships and networks
- Identify a stakeholder plan early.

Theme 4 – development

Subordinate themes:

- Developing potential and confidence by tapping into inner resources
- To be at your best – meaning, purpose and values
- Source feedback mechanisms for personal stretch and growth
- Identify own authentic leadership approach
- Develop others' potential – empowerment and autonomy of team
- Letting go and delegating
- Gain new insights (light bulb moments)
- Career – managing from here to the future
- Sustainable learning – action learning in role and transferrable application of tools and techniques.

While these results are applicable to all the leaders, it is worth noting they exist on a continuum; the variations will now be discussed in the following chapters with illustrative examples from the transcripts.

7 Time to think

The starting point for the leaders is thinking time. This is essential in order for leaders to create reflective space in a new and very busy work environment. They work with a coach to add value as they think and plan. Through questions from the coach critical thinking is evoked in the leader, which broadens the lens in order to more fully see the new landscape.

Challenges and opportunities are explored. Thinking and assumptions are challenged and possible options can be critically considered. Challenge from the coach widens the lens of possibilities as the leader starts to consider a new future.

The first subordinate theme 'finding your feet in a new dynamic' relates to the leader's experience of orientation around the new role. This is where the leader starts to explore and see the new features, as they navigate this new landscape and understand the new dynamics.

Finding your feet in a new dynamic

All the leaders acknowledged the unique things they were discovering as they navigated their way into their new role.

Jim

Jim acknowledges the 'not knowing' stage, either about the role or what the future holds for his career beyond this role.

> So it was quite a different role. Both in terms of the shape of the team and the size of the team.

> Probably not knowing the role as well is the core thing and also being at a stage of my career development where I am not quite sure of what I am going to do next.

> It's a different landscape and also it's a different time career wise.

> So they are the kind of things that definitely evolved and making me think myself about how I think about the role and what is in the role.

Kate

Kate had just started in her new role before going on maternity leave. On her return from maternity leave almost a year later she is finding her way again in a new role and is dealing with a different dynamic as well. She is finding her way about again.

> We were quite clear in terms of what we were trying to work on and then I was at that point adjusting to a new role even at that level.

> I met her [coach] about six weeks after I started so I came back at the end of June and I met her through the middle of August. August would be a traditionally quiet month here and I would feel that a lot of . . . still really trying to find my feet in terms of the role.

> The dynamic between the ourselves and the regulated entities and the policy makers had changed significantly so it was dealing with a different dynamic as well. So, we were kind of finding our feet in terms of that new dynamic.

> I just had to ensure the whole new dynamic was working effectively and it didn't become a problem and ensure there was an escalation of the key issues.

Kevin

> When you got into the bigger organization, it's a bit of a more challenging thing.

John

> But now I was moving to a new division with different functional areas linked to market so the markets experience was useful, but that wasn't necessarily what I was working on, so I needed to . . .

> I suppose I am making a transition and it's a transition both from where I worked in financial markets and risk under X Company. I never worked in financial regulation. I was making a transition across to a totally different division but basically no one would really know me and so I felt in that context that really what I could do with is something that could help me.

Paul

Even though Paul has held previous leadership roles, he acknowledges the step change to director level and he identifies the aspects he needs to pay attention to from different angles as he makes the necessary adjustments to his new role.

> It was all quite new territory for me in terms of a new role and moving into a director position and those accountabilities and there was a lot going on in the day job as you can imagine with all of that.

I suppose getting to grips with a new role at quite a senior level and the accountabilities and dealing with all the adjustment to that. So, I had been a line manager before. So it wasn't new, but this was on a bigger scale and more senior people reporting into me. And I had been on leadership teams before, but now I was on more senior leadership teams in this role, so all that adjustment there and dealing with some new processes, systems, getting up to speed, learning about stuff that I needed to learn about, quickly building a lot of relationships, you know vertically, horizontally.

Marion

So, at the beginning it was very much a sounding board and a check in place and a finding my way.

Discipline of reflecting to create value in a very busy world

The leaders referred to their busy work environments and the emerging urgency of their new role. At the same time they signalled a need to create discipline, which will allow them time to reflect and create value for the business.

Helena realizes that the reflection time will allow her to focus on a way forward that will deliver results for her, both in the short term and in the longer term. She keeps the end game in mind.

Helena

Giving me the space to do that because in a very busy world it is extremely difficult to do that. And I suppose beyond that, as well, it is not just about the coaching meeting, what it does is that it instils that discipline in you – every day I take a half an hour where I just sit and I just reflect myself around my plans or what I have done or how I am feeling. It just instils that discipline.

Also looking at where I could bring the value now. Where I am now, where I wanted to be in the future, but where I can hit the ground running and where I can bring that value while I plan and bring my team and my immediate team on board to develop a plan into the future. And to get results, at the end of the day there's a job to be done here, it's not all woolly and fluffy and while it's nice talking and taking time out to reflect but I suppose what it is about is . . . what coaching allows you to do is to take the time out so that you can do the reflection to deliver the results so there is an end game in mind.

I would see it [working with the coach] as a hugely enriching experience and anyone in my view to think that it is taking time away from you is foolish, because what it does is it creates so much value in other ways and so much . . . It just creates some other avenues for you and it creates that space for yourself which is kind of invaluable really.

Jim

Jim is naturally task focused and through coaching has seen the value of reflection, as he considers his engagement with others, which he sees as very valuable for him.

Just . . . taking time away . . . making time away from day to day work to think about how you can progress to be a better leader in your role and that is something I value very much. I have a very busy role – as such as there is a lot going on and I can very easily get caught up with meetings and tasks and all of that.

So, I think getting into coaching gives me a very good . . . it's almost a good bit of time and it is a constant reminder that to focus on that development of potential and growth and to maybe think about things that are in the back of my head or in the middle of my head and know that I should be doing. It brings me back to what I should be doing this day, this week. It keeps me honest to myself.

I was very much focused on tasks and deliverables and deadlines and that was important in the role as well, but coaching did it to some extent the first time and it is definitely doing it again this time. It is making me realize the benefit and freeing myself up from the day to day, to spend a bit of time reflecting and considering things and planning how to engage with people before I do and to see that there is huge merit in that, and that is not me taking time out sitting about blue-sky gazing. That is incredibly useful.

John

You can underestimate that when you leave the office and you go to a different place and you talk about yourself and you're listened to and that sort of environment . . . that's good in a way.

Marion

Marion sees the value of creating the space to get a reality check on her own thoughts as she works through things.

I think it just gave me the space to be able to explore sometimes things that were not that big of a challenge until you discussed them and put them out on the table and then you think they are a challenge. It gave me the space to work through things. It gave me clarity, visibility and results. All of which coaching is all about. You do it all yourself. It's just someone sitting across from you asking all the right questions, you know, which is pretty powerful.

I think you have to be more disciplined and I think it's funny because we did discuss this the last day and she talked about the fact that she does some self-coaching herself and she shared with me her coaching questions and it is really about me having the discipline for me to book myself into this room and do a coaching session for myself. But I think that probably is quite hard but I think doing it with colleagues . . . I think I can do it with people that I trust.

Have thinking and assumptions challenged

All of the leaders indicated the immense value of having their thinking and assumptions challenged by the coach.

Both Jim and Kevin make reference to the fact that it feels like looking in the mirror.

Paul would have preferred a stronger challenge from the coach in order to get more of a stretch.

Helena views the challenge as a way to look at situations differently and more objectively in terms of herself or others' behaviours. Jim sees the questions as a way to keep himself on track and to be more accountable to himself.

Helena

. . . and the opportunity to explore your own thinking and to have somebody we will say am, challenge that thinking in a very non . . . in a very kind of different way, erm but I suppose for me it really is giving me that time to stand back and reflect and look at myself, my behaviours, look at situations and others' behaviours and I suppose very objectively analyse myself as well, but giving me the space to do that, because in a very busy world it is extremely difficult to do that.

Jim

What I liked about it the first time was what the coach did. It's like putting up the mirror to you and asking you the questions that you are asking yourself and maybe not verbalizing them and asking them explicitly and I like the fact that it made me be more accountable to myself.

Kate

There is a challenge from her to me which I find helpful in the context of you know of certain assumptions or statements that I would make . . . just for me to check those. So, she would say to me, so why do you think that? Or have you done any work around that? And maybe I would go . . . em . . . no probably I haven't so she actually gets me to challenge my own assumptions around maybe – perceived roadblocks is too strong a word – so I would say perceived just things I feel I would have to work my way around, whereas actually if I challenged that assumption it is not a big . . . I don't have to work my way around it . . . I can just go through it if that makes sense. Isn't that a strange thing probably to say . . . ? So, I find she has a very good way of just challenging some of the things that I am saying.

Kevin

In the middle of the thing I think is where most of the work was done where you are really being challenged, the questions that the coach was giving me were really challenging me.

You know what I mean, the conversations, you know it's like looking in the mirror. You know it is, and they are doing it in such a way to get the best out of you, but sometimes it doesn't feel like that in the session.

John

John's awareness has been heightened through having his assumptions challenged and he can see that link to his behaviour that was limiting him.

I think what the coaching addressed was the way I view myself and the assumptions I was making about myself, how these assumptions were manifesting themselves in behaviour and how these behaviours were limiting my ability to progress in my impact or whatever so.

Paul

Paul wanted a stronger challenge and requested that the coach be more challenging. He felt he would have got more value from a more challenging style of engagement.

And I was conscious of that and took it seriously, but did I really extract as much value as I could have from it? I am not sure I did. I certainly could have for the first half and then I sort of did stop and think and I did say to my coach that I felt it was too safe, it was too punctual and I said that to her. And I asked her and my request was for her to be more provocative, more challenging, don't give me an easy ride because I said 'I don't think it is your fault because I am probably maybe participating in this conversation probably in a way that is 80 per cent of what it should be from my perspective'.

More of a challenge, yes and earlier on, but because I was so busy spinning so many plates, it wasn't . . . a . . . but in hindsight I do have a few regrets and if I was coaching somebody about it, I would say really . . . and I did coaching some other folks and I would be really clear up front, this is a fantastic opportunity, so almost over-emphasize in your own mind what you want to get out of it, so I think my coach who in ways was fantastic, because her style was very engaging. I mean, other people, I know their coaches practically thumped them, you know it was like in a psychological sense, like came in and said 'Don't talk shite', you know, and not in those words, but really kind of shook them and I know some folks really appreciated that and felt wow it was great. They really grabbed me by the ankles and turned me upside down and really put me through the wringer. My coach would never ever do that. And even when I made a challenge around the provocation bit, she did shift the emphasis but still . . . in a way it probably let me off the hook a bit in that 'did she really cause me to challenge me' as much as I could have and should have. She probably didn't. I have to take some of the blame for that because they . . . it's like any counsellor or coach, it's not about . . . you know you are helping the person to figure it out themselves ultimately, the coach does not have to figure it out for them. So, I don't expect her to figure it all out for me. But could she have at an earlier stage said to me, 'Paul I think you are treading water a bit here, are you really grabbing this and wrestling with some of the issues?' So, in ways, I got an awful lot from the conversation over the year.

Richard

Richard was open to the challenges and saw them in a positive light, but got frustrated when the solution to an issue that seemed the most visible wouldn't work in his organization. He refers to it all as a bit messy.

Initially it was . . . I won't say unnerving but it was a bit outside of my comfort zone. I didn't know this person and we started to get into quite personal conversations. So, it took me a while to feel at ease and I am not used to being challenged to the extent that this lady challenged me as well. And to be asked and the question kept coming back: Why? Why? Why do you want this? Why do you want that and I suppose, to be honest, I would have been arrogant would be a wrong word but I would have got a senior enough position quite young, so I had been thinking I am doing very well and erm . . . this person quite categorically put me in the box and said it is not really about the age that you are, but when you have this opportunity to progress, seize it because you may not get that opportunity or clear run of luck or whatever in different periods of your life. So, I suppose that is the specifics but I was kind of interested in those push backs and challenge, so I found the whole thing quite challenging. Yes, challenging is the right word but in a good way.

So they would ask, they would probe and maybe they kind of helped clear my thoughts but I had come very clearly to the answer so I would own the answer but then I would go with, well, that clearly won't work, no, no, no and that's where it got a bit messy. Does that make sense to you?

Create space to think and plan to develop vision and direction

It is important for leaders to take the time to create a vision that provides clarity and direction, both for the leader, the team and the wider organization. This sets the tone for what is being focused on and delivered within the business.

Leaders referenced the importance of vision and direction. Helena as a leader understands the energy that leaders need to bring, as they bring the vision to their team. This allows people to decide if they will follow the leader and get on the bus.

Helena

But also setting out the long-term vision and creating that vision for people and getting the energy or having or bringing the energy I should say, that people get excited and enthused about getting on the bus with you.

Jim

Jim's approach is to get explicit clarity by writing out what he wants to have happening in his future in a year's time.

At the beginning, I think it was very much getting me to sit back and think strategically about where I wanted to be, so we did this exercise taking a helicopter view of where I wanted to be in 12 months and again it explicitly made me sit down and say what exactly do I want things to look like. And then put steps in place to follow and to get there. So, the beginning was very much making that time to picture that vision and the middle was how are we progressing, how can we shift things to focus around a little bit better to see how we can make it happen and at the end it gave me a great sense of satisfaction and achievement and validation of the value of the coaching. I could see the picture that I wanted and I absolutely got there and I even did it a bit better.

Paul

Paul as a leader is focused on understanding what the future needs are that will influence what are the right things to be busy with in the business today.

For me there is something around, to distil it down, it is that sense of being busy at the right things and therefore to do that, you have got to stand in the future. You have got to take that longer-term view. If you stand too long in the future, you stand the risk of the day to day, you lose that focus of today, tomorrow, next week so you end up almost naval gazing so there is a balance to be had there.

Marion

Marion knows that creating the future picture is not the most natural for her, so she will need some support in this area.

I always say give me something and tell me what you want me to get to and I have no problem getting all the people together to get us there, but actually coming up with 'where' there is, is a bit more challenging. So, the longer-term strategic vision of it.

Other sessions I might have looked at were my strategy, my vision for the cluster and things like that.

Widen the lens with critical thinking to explore challenges and opportunities

Weighing up information and taking a more critical look at scenarios allows a wider lens in terms of potential opportunities and solutions. Kevin sees how limitations around time and thinking can limit the possibilities and solutions to which a person potentially has access. Through challenging oneself to take a more critical look at scenarios, this can lead to better solutions, as more aspects have been considered. As Kevin notes, especially in relation to considering if others are 'on the train' with you.

Helena

Value add. Huge value add. And directional, I would say. in the context, I suppose, of . . . in a traditional way, she is not coming up with all the answers for me. She is just kind of challenging some of your assumptions and mainly thinking about possible ways forward for you and you come up with that together. Yes, directional and value add.

Kevin

And I suppose the other really big thing is to think wider than you normally think. I think that . . . so you might think you have three options, but actually challenge yourself to say there are six to evaluate. Now in some instances you don't have the time. You just might have to go. But I think the general thing is, it's a good thing to be reflective, sit back, think about it and then ultimately you have to make a decision, but it's really better if everyone is on the train.

So, in all those sessions it was about laying out the options available and more importantly to keep all the options open. So, if you are there and you are trying to transition to a new role and you have your heart set on X, but X isn't available, then what is Y and Z? And then we discussed those and the pros and cons of those and then maybe in three months' time, we will come back and see is that still the status or has something else come onto the table.

Paul

Paul uses his critical thinking to consider the challenges and opportunities of the future and to find better ways to get ready for them.

So I suppose I always have had a restlessness and an interest in looking beyond the status quo and thinking OK, so what should we be doing or thinking about differently in the context of being better set up for the future and being better able to operate to deal with the challenges and opportunities that arise, etc. So that is what I like to do, so when I work myself or when I am doing a bit of work with others.

On reflection afterwards, I sort of felt 'Do you know what if I was her, I would have been more challenging'. I would have said 'Hold on Paul, based on our previous conversation a month ago, whenever, I am not sure you are really addressing the issue or the opportunity or the challenge. I think you are . . .' So probably, in that sense, she could have caused me to be more challenging of myself in terms of some of the opportunities, some of the risks I may be perceived. And I think I probably left something behind in that process. I am not hung up on it because overall it was a great process.

Marion

I think it just gave me the space to be able to explore sometimes things that were not that big of a challenge until you discussed them and put them out on the table and then you think they are a challenge. It gave me the space to work through things. It gave me clarity, visibility and results. All of which coaching is all about. You do it all yourself. It's just someone sitting across from you asking all the right questions you know which is pretty powerful.

8 Clarity and focus

The second main theme is clarity and focus and this is where the leader starts to open up and develop a pathway for the future they want to create

A psychologically safe environment with trust and openness

Probably the most critical aspect of working with a coach is the sense of trust that is created in that relationship. This allows a sense of safety, which allows the leader to open upto discussing whatever is on their mind. Any reservations here will limit the potential within the coaching process.

All of the leaders spoke about how important that trust with their coach was for them. The trust determined most of the potential value that could derive from the coaching interaction. It allowed openness on behalf of leaders, where they could put whatever they wanted to discuss on the table. It was the leader's agenda: unlike other relationships in organizations where others' needs or agendas can be more of the focus. It is a unique relational space where the leader can feel supported.

Helena

It has to be a two-way thing. So, you have to be able to go and sell your soul . . . well, not sell your soul, but put your soul on the table and if you are feeling emotional and upset about something, you need to be able to share that and that needs to be a safe environment for you to do so. So, if you don't completely have that relationship with your coach and you don't trust them enough, I don't think you are going to get what you need to get out of coaching.

John

. . . and just in that kind of space like in that environment where you could basically say whatever you wanted. That was the most useful part of it.

Kevin

You know. So sometimes it's actually the stuff outside the core that is impacting on the core. You know if it is something to do with family, that's not necessarily related to work but if you can solve the family bit you can actually then have your mind clear or whatever. So, I think the first time I had the experience with the coach, there was a trust piece so it was late session 2 before I say, even though I knew I got on well with her at the chemistry check.

I suppose you know at the start there is that whole dynamic around the trust, you know, how open am I going to be with the coach. So, in other words, am I going to lay every single piece or am I going to stick to. . . the core issue is. You know.

Marion

For me, my view always on these things is unless you give them everything pretty much, they are not going to be able to coach you very well.

At the front end, I feel it was very much like a safety blanket or something and it was just a really safe space to come into, a place to bounce ideas around and to get feedback.

I think for me the coaching is really about having a really safe environment where you can open up about what your fears or concerns are or what are the challenges you are facing or things that you might have to encounter.

Kate

Yes, definitely. It's a very safe environment.

Kevin

Because at the end of the day, you know what I mean like, that trust piece, the coach is there. They are not there to question or evaluate you. They are there to sort of say . . . let's draw out a map here and let's look at the options, see which is the best for you at this moment in time.

Download and get structure on the issues

With so much new information coming at the new leaders the opportunity to stop and get context is important. Some of the leaders saw the value of getting their thoughts verbalized (which felt like a download) and this allowed them to consider their reality and put them in to a context with some structure. Through the support of the coach, this allowed visibility that facilitated greater understanding and response choice.

Helena

The opportunity to create clarity of thought and now as I move into the middle it is about putting structure around that.

I suppose it helped me to see the woods from the trees and attend to the important versus the unimportant and to compartmentalize things and to focus on you know obviously short, medium and long term.

Kate

And I think the coach is very good at structuring what the issues are because sometimes I just download a lot of information to the coach and then sometimes I can put some structure on it in terms of there are three things I want to discuss with you and I have probably found that as I have done more and more coaching, I am much more of, this is what I want to get out of this session, but initially I probably felt that it was downloading a lot of stuff and she would put some structure in terms of OK, well, I think that is related to that and this is the area we need to think about, maybe you would think about working on.

Yes, directional and value add and I found it very structured and both my experiences with the coaches, what I find is amazing is when you do that download, so as I said I have got more structured in terms of how I should go with these three areas I think I should talk to you about today. I find coaches great in the context of you can do that download. It's amazing at the end of the session they have managed to deal with all of those things. They are thinking all the time in the context of all of that, maybe, noise and how we might kind of deal with that. I am always very surprised by that, like that is amazing, like they can tick off all of those things. Yeah, so that's very good.

Kevin

I thought that was that bit that . . . so . . . I knew all those things myself, but they were all in a muddle. I thought the beauty of the coach was she was able to take them down, prioritize them, evaluate them with me and, at the end of the day, I was doing all the evaluation, but it was just the structure that was used, that was really helpful.

If I have a coaching intervention and I have a session with my coach, I can park all that baggage or all that concerns and just get on with the day job. So, I think that's a huge thing sometimes that people feel that an intervention whether it's a coach or a mentoring relationship, it allows you to get a really honest conversation and maybe clarify a few things around your own values and then park that or keep working on where you need to work on, being strategic and then come back and get on with the day job. Well that to me . . . that's our experience with a high IQ organization.

John

I found it a big support in terms of being able to sort of go to a room and air what was going on with me.

Because I wasn't quite clear on certain things and so she did facilitate on things that I didn't know . . . I found it useful but I guess I would have found it more useful if I was really clear about what I wanted to work on. I found it a big support in terms of being able to sort of go to a room and air what was going on with me.

Richard

The middle part of it was about kind of problem-solving, problem-solving big bottleneck blocker issues that are stopping me getting the way of where I need to get to for the business.

Broaden perspective by developing a wider lens

The opportunity for leaders to gain a wider lens with more perspective is key to how they will see and deal with the world. Coaches, through questioning, can tap into deeper-level thinking, which generates different perspectives that can open up new ways of viewing issues and creating alternative ways of dealing with things that had not been considered before.

The leaders gave examples of how they have benefited from gaining different perspectives with some guidance from their coach.

Helena

I find it helps me look at things differently and it is about looking at things differently. And it is about looking at things differently.

I suppose what it created for me was the ability to pause for thought, to look at things differently, to look at them from different perspectives.

Kate

You know so, in the first instance I would find having an objective perspective on the issues you are struggling with or need some guidance on very helpful.

What I would say also is that I set very high standards for myself so that is good probably if you are my boss erm . . . but sometimes it might not be great if you are working with me so, sometimes good is good enough from that perspective so I think I have got to learn that that might not be exactly how I would do things.

As I am settling more into the role, I am kind of seven months in it now, like new things are arising for me that we are discussing and I always get her perspective on those as well. It's not about revisiting the same old issues. So, the last session was three new things.

Kevin

It's trying to get the magic of the person coming up with the idea rather than you telling them. Yet you have to be pushy enough to get them to a point where they will think in a slightly different way, slightly outside the box. It broadens their thinking and it stretches it out.

I think it opened my eyes to a wider lens. I think that's the real, real bit that . . . you know we are all here busy in the today, the now, whenever but really if we are going to be great leaders, we need to be out, further out here.

You know what we are having in this whole performance management, this conversation which is the 'what' and the 'how'. So, you know I could have done a great 'what' and the team is dead at the end of the year. You know whereas if I look after the 'how', then I will get the 'what' done. You can have a great year and have the team dead or you can have a great year and have the team energized to take it forward. It's long term and the lens was widened.

John

I was making a transition across to a totally different division but basically no one would really know me and so I felt in that context that really what I could do with is something that could help me tap into my own sort of resources and help me to sort of look at things from a different perspective. What I was really looking towards in the profiles was someone that worked with people who were making transitions. So, I was conscious that somebody that would be able to help me to work on that transition across both in terms of managing myself and then, you know, having a sort of planned progressive transition across the line, that I was managing that transition well.

Not life and death issues but there still were, shall we say, the little nagging issues that interrupt your flow in terms of work so it was good to be able to come to a place and hear those issues in a way and maybe have my assumptions challenged around them and then be pushed towards solutions rather than sort of focusing on the issues themselves and to get different perspectives. So, I found that part very useful.

Marion

I think I have figured a lot out over the year anyway while working with her and about, you know, certain things and seeing individuals, for example, my boss in different lights and realizing that there are different views, different opinions. It is not always one is right and one is wrong.

Operate at the right level for impact and influence

It is important for the new leader to manage their profile as they take on the new role. The capabilities for a leadership role are different from those required for a content expert with a high level of technical expertise. Therefore, leaders need to consider how they show up and can influence and create an impact with the organization. Many of the leaders referred to making an impact and having influence. They gave examples from communication style to letting go and removing their focus on the operations side of the work. More awareness around their style of communications, their behaviours, networking and managing upwards with more senior managers were specifically mentioned.

Kate

So I found her very, very helpful in the context of just kind of, as you become more senior in the organization, how you stop doing the things you had done before because otherwise if you keep doing those, you are still operating at the same level and you are not growing and making sure you are really operating at the right level with your peers and the director and things like that.

I think it is important to understand what are people talking about there, which is that I suppose to try and anticipate things a little bit more in advance and trying to raise it up a bit at the right level in that context with particular issues.

So, I think you have to continue to work on that and also, I observe, so people I respect, people I have worked with previously, how they operate at committees in terms of their interventions and I suppose I have tried to learn from them in the context of how you interject when you want to make a point, what points you might make, what ones you might leave and, you know, things like that. So that is one aspect of it.

Another piece of feedback I would have got as well is, in terms of my communication style, and this is something that I have been very conscious of is that not to be too elaborate in my communication and to be conscious of who my audience is. So more internally than externally, I think.

John

My current coaching arrangement is around the transition and the impact I will have in my new directorate.

The other thing that she talked about which I thought was very good. She caught me being longwinded and then she stopped me and she said 'now this is what I am hearing, is that your intention' and it was just those sorts of impact and influence pieces, being able to reframe. So, to hear how she was experiencing me was very useful as well.

My impact and influence particularly with senior management because at times I may talk around things and I give more of a context than what is needed. I may not be as direct or point focused or you know . . . there are three things here, the first is this . . . the second is this and the third is this . . . I don't always approach things in that way. I would give more context than what I need to. I may be over staff-focused, but the main thing is the impact and influence on senior managers, being able to articulate myself in short bursts and land the message that needs to be landed, but do that sort of in a concise way.

Jim

I guess I have a natural interest in how my words and actions impacted on those around me and the different personalities and the psychology of those people within the team.

Marion

Definitely when I was crafting the leadership story. That was probably the highlight, that I came out with a story that I was so happy with and went around and told nine different markets at that stage. Erm . . . I would have come up with a version of it, but I don't think it would have been as strong. I don't think it would have been as focused and I just think it wouldn't have been as impactful.

Gain clarity and focus on priorities and develop a plan

Clarity and focus on priorities is key to being effective to ensure the leader is working on the right things and the important things.

Helena and Richard give examples of what it was like for them as they waded through much information. Richard describes some of this information as 'noise' that detracts from the important items that the leader needs to give his or her focus and attention to. Helena describes it as seeing the 'woods from the trees'.

Helena

When I got into the coaching engagement, I suppose in this particular role now. There is so much to be done, you know. There's a million priorities. It helped me see the woods from the trees and attend to the important versus the unimportant.

Jim

I think I could go back to that and that was really what I wanted at the start and I think there was clarity in that and this time around again probably getting to that stage of clarity this is now what I want out of this, I want this out of this engagement, which would have taken a bit more work, and that is fine with me because I knew I was throwing a lot of balls in the air, so the clarity at the beginning – whether that comes in the 1st session or the 3rd session – I think is one of the most beneficial aspects of it. After that it is a bit of . . . well, what are the steps to get to and do the steps whereas I think the hardest part is figuring out what I want at the end.

Kate

So I find the coach very helpful in the context of focusing your mind in terms of your presence in meetings, you have very little time to prepare how you might do that erm because before you would be in the detail because you are the subject matter expert in all of that kind of stuff.

Paul

Because people can ask me and pull me into this piece of work and that piece of work and a bit of strategy work there and I like it. I am interested in it and you could spend your whole day doing it. The thing is I have other staff and I need to focus on their . . . they are probably the two main areas, but there are others.

But oftentimes, in my head, I have a belief that lots of companies have failed or relationships have failed, it's not because people set out to fail, but they are often busy at the wrong things. And what I like to try and do is say how can we be busy at the right things.

Marion

In the middle then it was more so actually planning 'and this is what I am planning and helping me shape things'. You know. One of the comments my coach would have given me is that she feels it is quite easy coaching me because I am quite open to it and I sort of know what I want to do anyway. Sometimes it is probably literally that assurance and somebody to talk it out loud with and map it out. We stood in this room many times with a flip chart and mapped things out.

Richard

And the other one which is very important is focussing on the knitting, getting the three to five things and focus on them and get rid of the noise.

But it gave me a real understanding that there is only so much big change you should take on at any one time in order for you to do it properly, in order for you to flourish. So, it is one thing I am very cognizant of in my work and my home life, only a certain amount of things are taken on at any one time because it was way too much. And I got that . . . [pause] I wouldn't have . . . I didn't get that clarity elsewhere.

Check-in to review and revise

Regular check-ins with a coach brings with it accountability for the leader. It also gave the coaches visible indicators of progress or new areas that now needed attention. Many of the leaders describe the value of that check-in as they navigated the change and reviewed progress. It allowed them to stop and reflect and see where they were now and where they were moving towards. It created headspace to consider any necessary adjustments before they moved onwards again. They were now navigating their journey with a compass they had created through working with their coach.

Helena

Am I looking at this the right way and you are trying to listen to everybody you could get the whole thing derailed and with the coaching it helps you to stand back and realize where you are and then go back and . . . what I set out at the beginning is where I am now, where I wanted to be in three to six months' time, where I wanted to be in a year's time or whatever and how . . . or am I moving further away and what adjustments do I have to make, do I have to expedite things? Are there individuals I have to work with? Do I have to do somethings off line? Do I have to seek . . . from the rest of the SMT and also I suppose because this is my own team.

Jim

. . . and the middle was how are we progressing, how can we shift things to focus around a little bit better to see how we can make it happen.

Kate

I am quite structured and organized but having said that sometimes, I just find that the sessions that you just do a lot of talking initially and then we take a pause and then we just go back and revisit each of the items.

John

I found the check-in and actually where I would say 'this is what I have done'. There was a certain discipline around all of that that was obviously useful.

. . . and then the follow-up and what have you done since the last time. What worked and what didn't work and just in that kind of space like in that environment where you could basically say whatever you wanted. That was the most useful part of it.

Marion

So, at the beginning it was very much a sounding board and a check in place and a finding my way.

Richard

I would bring specific real-life examples of issues I was having at work and we would tease them out as a case study and in the following three or four or even five weeks I would look at dealing with that issue before I would go back to her so that I would have something to look at and look forward to as well.

Working smart and sustaining focus and energy

Working smart will mean different things to different people. If it is to be linked to managing focus and energy, it is useful to figure out what your strengths are and use them to work more efficiently.

The leaders considered different options here. It meant utilizing both their own and others' resources to best advantage. From considering approaches such as preparation before meetings, taking a more overview perspective instead of detail-centred, delegation, ensuring the team are working effectively, managing the in-box (emails), self-regulation and managing are all ways that help build more resilience for the road ahead.

Helena

Again, it can be very impactful when this is all great and energized, but how do you maintain it? How do you stay resilient, how do you keep that energy going and I think that is where coaching comes into its own as well.

Jim

There is a danger a little bit of being I know it all and you know it all better yourself and moving to a team now where you don't know anyone's role.

So, I think I can improve on that and I can definitely improve in being a bit more disciplined in how I work, as well in that I could be better to let people do the task themselves and stay totally out of it. But I think a certain amount of it will evolve more naturally now that I am six months into the role, I am more confident with what is going on and I don't have to spend more time understanding everything so I can sort through what is the stuff I can let go and what do I need to be more on top of so they are a couple of things.

Kate

I have also found her extremely beneficial in the context of . . . I think you know it's pretty important as you move up the organization, in terms of your capacity, so in terms of how you focus on the right things, how you can pre-pare efficiently for whatever is coming at you, how you ensure that your team is working efficiently and effectively and how you can ensure you are adding value and not get overwhelmed too much. So, I find her particularly beneficial in that context.

I would say I am very resilient. I do have huge capacity I think and I sometimes think that can be a negative too. I can sometimes take that to the limit.

So I find the coach very helpful in the context of focusing your mind in terms of your presence in meetings, you have very little time to prepare how you might do that erm because before you would be in the detail because you are the subject matter expert in all of that kind of stuff. Trusting your team, you know. So I found her very, very helpful in the context of just kind of, as you become more senior in the organization, how you stop doing the things you had done before, because otherwise, if you keep doing those, you are still operating at the same level and you are not growing and making sure you are really operating at the right level with your peers and the director and things like that and I suppose that you can have confidence in the fact that I haven't read everything but I have thought about a couple of salient points that I want to raise here so basically having confidence in the context of shorter time to prepare and be more efficient about how you operate yourself. So very helpful in that regard.

Kevin

. . . and I think that's where the coach . . . because sometimes like that, you can sort of, you can let that be seen and you just need to be careful about . . . You do, because there is a long game here and the long game here is like the emotional intelligence. It is how can I hold myself in very uncomfortable spaces.

Richard

I became less detail centric. I became more overview, strategic. I delegated a bit more but as a consequence of this I found myself less busy because I would have always been the one previously to get down to the detail and make sure that I knew as much as everyone else and I do well to fill up eight hours now.

Ah . . . I don't get stressed. I would have an awful lot of self-belief in me and my team. I can get an awful lot done quickly. I don't procrastinate, so my way of working is I have to have an empty inbox.

9

Collaborate with others

The third main theme is collaborate with others and this is essential for leaders as they partner with others to achieve the desired goals of the business. The world of work has changed with leadership and autonomy being devolved to the frontline teams. New leadership models are evolving and it is more critical than ever that leaders see the value of collaboration.

Collaborate with new leadership team (leader of leaders) to develop one vision

New leaders need to collaborate with their direct reports, who are also leaders of others, in order to work to a shared vision with shared goals.

Helena and Kate acknowledge the contribution of their management team to developing the shared goals and setting out their performance expectations. They realize that the business delivery will come through the teams.

Helena

I also want to bring them together as a management team. I want them to be seen as such. I want them to shine and I want them to feel that they are completely empowered and that's all nice language, but that's actually what needs to happen as well, so that they can be successful because this isn't about me. It's about them because they are the real leaders of the next layer down and so on.

Kate

Secondly, to ask them what do they see that is good here, what do they think we could improve on and then give them an understanding of what I expect, because I have people here pretty much all at a manager level, so I don't have a huge mix of grade structures so there is a big expectation in terms of leadership and delivery from my perspective. So, the challenge now I would see is that people understand what is acceptable from my perspective and, also, I would think my deputy, she and I would be singing from the same hymn sheet in terms of a standard and particularly given the level they are at, turnaround and adherence to deadlines, things like that, adding value.

And, also, what I would say is a real clear expectation that people take up ownership and responsibility for their work.

Kevin

And also, myself to transition out of . . . I know the job more than the individuals that I have appointed, so how do I transition myself to give them their space to grow technically, but also to grow as people managers and leaders?

Flex approach for effective interactions and engagement with different personalities

While leaders are commercially driven, knowing what their actual behaviour is like in the organization and understanding the reactions from others is valuable, as without that insight, the leader can risk bruising people unnecessarily or working in isolation.

Engagement and interactions are influenced by a person's own experience of the world. There is no reality except the reality we create. Taking the time to find out where others are coming from lets the other person feel understood. This is often an aspect of emotional intelligence and is important when building new relationships.

Kate has found coaching a good support and a reminder to her that she has good interactions.

Kevin notes Myers Briggs as a useful lens through which to view personalities and differences as he navigates the journey.

Richard acknowledges that as a leader the technical issues can be straightforward but the people issues can be tricky. Through coaching he has found ways to bring about an appropriate response that gives him the answer or the fuel, as he describes it, to get to the result that he needs.

Helena

I see the challenges that there are and I also see the opportunities and I talk in a language of opportunity and motivation rather than challenge and issues.

And then there's a whole, so preparation for your meetings when you are having your one-on-ones with people is whatever, a set of questions to ask that are non-confrontational. Like I think 'Why'? is a very confrontational question, because people feel they have to defend something then whereas it's just about . . . So, I think the tools and techniques they give you is just a way of thinking about the questions you are going to ask and how you are going to ask them or the language you will use.

Jim

Others were attuned to the more psychological aspects of it and that was more where I was leaning towards. I actually found through some of the work that was required for the interviews we did for senior manager tests, psychology is part of that and I found that really useful and really interesting. I suppose it's a part of managing or leading that I was always interested in. I guess I have a natural interest in how my words and actions impacted on those around me and the different personalities and the psychology of those people within the team.

Making me think myself about how I think about the role and what is in the role and definitely this time more of a slant towards the people side and towards the psychology of all of it, the types of personalities that you are engaging with.

And I guess, even now as I interact with the team I am engaging with now, I would have a good sense already of what general personality types they may be and some people are more transparent and some people are more guarded and I just need to interact with them the right way.

Especially when I started off in a position where I thought I was a good listener. I thought they knew where I was coming from. I probably did try but I didn't actually act on it. So, I think I can improve on that.

I am interested in people and I think as a manager and a leader of people that's a natural strength, because you are more inclined to think about where people are coming from and to think about how a change or a request or a task might be interpreted by someone because I am more recently promoted and have come through the ranks, so I am also more probably aware as to . . . There are certain real high achievers on my team and they want to get promoted themselves and I have a personal understanding where people are at in their lives and so I think a strength might be trying to understand where people are coming from and spending time considering that when I trying to engage and work with them. So that aspect of relationship building is important to me.

It is making me realize the benefit and freeing myself up from the day-to-day to spend a bit of time reflecting and considering things and planning how to engage with people before I do and to see that there is huge merit in that and that is not me taking time out sitting about blue-sky gazing. That is incredibly useful. That gets me the answer from the engagement that we need to progress with whatever aspect of work I want to do.

Kate

. . . and just as a frame of reference so I would get articles from her as well and she would send me on things I could think about so just remind yourself in terms of your interactions.

Kevin

Whereas it's a bit like the Myers Briggs, does it really hugely matter which of the 16 boxes you are in as long as you are aware of it and what it means when you are interacting with someone else? And you know you are here as an extravert and someone else is here as an introvert, somehow you both have to move a little bit but if you are over there and they are over there, there is always going to be tension. So, it is helpful to navigate those journeys.

Richard

They [coach] had more impact for me when I was dealing with personnel issues. The more and more I have been involved in leadership roles, the more I have understood that the work itself is not rocket science. It's dealing with the people that can be the tricky one. Some of the most mundane small little things would come up and become huge issues and I became a lot more resolute in terms of determining what the right thing was and doing it in a kind of an appropriate manner and sticking by my guns and I dealt with some very tricky HR issues using some of the coaching learnings I had as kind of fuel to get to where I needed to get to.

Navigate the journey with the team and bring them on board

The journey and bringing people on board was mentioned in different ways by the leaders. Helena and Kevin specifically mentioned navigating the journey and about bringing people on board. Helen refers to taking a collective approach for moving forward.

Helena

. . . and bring my team on board to develop a plan for the future.

But how can you foster that and bring them together in one unit with such strength, power and, you know, with their own clarity of thought but, I suppose, lack of leadership is what they were really experiencing, you know.

I think the thing that really swung it I suppose was that erm . . . was first of all everyone was given a voice. That's all fine but when people went completely off the rails, it's back to how does that tie into our vision?

It was about that whole collective approach that until we all landed on the same spot, we weren't moving on.

. . . and we are on that journey, you know, I mean I was talking about journeys before, before that became such a tag line but we are on that road together, so that is one of the key areas.

Yes, and you all have to know that that is where you want to get to. And you don't all start at the same base point and you don't all agree on day one that you are going to end in the same space.

Jim

Definitely in the first coaching experience the time we spent initially thinking about where people were coming from, as I managed six people at that time from slightly varying backgrounds. Spending much more time thinking how they interacted with me at the start was very beneficial.

Kevin

And really the coaching was around navigating that journey as I interacted with the team, trying to sell to high IQ people that their emotions are important and raising that with the team and going back to the coach with how will I approach it? These guys are busy, these girls are busy, you know and that was really it. Trying to go on the journey . . . it's navigating it, you know what I mean. So erm . . . that was the first experience with the coaching.

It was a good team. It wasn't that I was doing it because the team was poor, I wanted to make a very good team great, so that is where we were starting from and they were happy to go on the journey. So that was really the bit, it was really touching in around that.

So, I think that is one of the big things that I think you know I might have an ambition to take the team, but unless I keep them fully informed all the way through the process, then they won't stay with you. Now in some instances, you know, not everyone on the team needs to be told every bit of detail or whatever.

But I think the general thing is it's a good thing to be reflective, sit back, think about it and then ultimately you have to make a decision but it's really better if everyone is on the train.

Setting expectations and performance conversations

Setting expectations and holding performance conversations with employees are key aspects of performance management process in organizations.

Kate is clear in terms of her criteria across the performance rankings and acknowledges that an employee can have a more limited view of the overall process. She also sees her role as leaders as an enabler to create opportunities for the employee to reach elevated performance measures.

Helena

So, I think absolutely all the coaching experience, all those questioning and listening and when I say challenging, I mean, just saying, you know let me be the devil's advocate and play the devil's advocate. And then when a decision needs to be made, make the decision, call it, move on, be consistent and be true to yourself as well. And sometimes they are not the easiest by any stretch of the imagination and they do take a lot of time and energy. I mean, it's exhausting. It's exhausting work but so worthwhile.

Kate

I think it is important for your manager to point that out and I think as part of performance assessment in my view and we are in the middle of the process at this stage in terms of moderation. Like how I would always personally and I think others would rank others in terms of the exceptional category, where they do more than what is expected of them in terms of their job because that is the contractual element. Doing the job well is not getting you into elevated performance categories. That is kind of your contract. And in terms of the scoring, we talked about this in terms of talent management. I think in some circumstances people don't understand that. They think that to be in the higher end of performance that it is OK to do your own job really well. Sometimes, that does not pan out that way because you have a peer group that you don't have visibility on and where we are comparing you against. And I suppose you have got to think how you differentiate yourself.

I would say it is not enabling people to maximize that as well. It's a really important part of what we do: we kind of have to say this is what we want. How is that going to happen for that person, maybe we have to throw other work their way. You have to enable people to have the chance to do that as well. So that is pretty important.

Kevin

You know what we are having in this whole performance management, this conversation which is the 'what' and the 'how'. So, you know, I could have done a great 'what' and the team is dead at the end of the year. You know whereas if I look after the 'how', then I will get the 'what' done. You can have a great year and have the team dead or you can have a great year and have the team energized to take it forward.

Think that's the thing as well having done the coaching. Now some of those conversations may be less adult to adult, (laugh) because the truth . . . I think you need to let people know that on an ongoing basis. So even the training or the opportunities for training or if someone is struggling, I am not sending them off on training and they are struggling to get their job done. So, you would try and explain some of those and you need to get back on track. But in a general sense it is rare that I find I ever went to the extreme of saying to someone I think you should leave this company. But that would be very unusual. No one wanted to work with the individual. They did leave.

Build new relationships and networks

Business gets delivered through people and relationships within organizational life are a key enabler to how effectively business gets done.

Many of the leaders note that building new relationships with their team members or new extended networks is important for them.

Jim realizes that he shouldn't take those relationships with his team for granted.

Helena invests in building trust within relationships through allowing trial and error.

Kevin notes the characteristic differences of type in personalities and the impact this can have in how relationships can play out.

Paul can see the need to build new networks but also acknowledges his level of discomfort in pursuing new networks. He is quite comfortable with his existing network so he needs to push outside of his comfort zone.

Marion is well aware of the value of relationships and the results she will get from investing in good relationships

Jim

It has probably opened my eyes a bit to that and also maybe just pointing me back towards both relationships with those key relationships with my team and not taking any of that for granted.

I probably had an early focus on relationships within the team but I didn't see the full opportunity in that from the start.

Helena

We are one part of the organization but we are also part of one organization and, yes, developing the relationships, as it is all about relationships and people.

. . . and also, to invest in people and to try things and let them fail. So, what, like. What you have done is that you have built a relationship.

So, I suppose I put a huge emphasis on relationships. I always would have had but I think the value of them and how easy they are to damage and how precious they are and how hard they are to build back up.

Kevin

And I suppose in that Myers Briggs it's strange. I am an extravert, my boss is an introvert and even managing that relationship is energy, whereas I am anxious to move and my boss is, yes, but we will have to replace you and the coach even trying to manage that relationship when it's an extravert vs an introvert.

Paul

If I am really being serious about my purpose, it's taking my networks further in terms of my relationships further, so I do it but I am probably too conservative about how hard I push that. My feedback recently from my line manager to a greater degree is . . . ? I will do it in relation to the networks I am comfortable in. Beyond that I am more . . . I don't not do it but I am more cautious with how I do it and the provocation is to do that more and to a higher degree.

Marion

So, for me it is all about relationships with people, to know the people, to recognize the good work and rewarding them. The results will then take care of themselves afterwards I feel and that has always worked for me.

Identify a stakeholder plan early

Knowing who your stakeholders are, analysing their needs and considering the type of interactions you will have with them is important as they will be key influencers and the leaders will have inter-dependencies with them in order to get work done.

The leaders did mention stakeholders in the interviews and Jim indicated he didn't have a sense of the level of stakeholders he would have and he realizes he will need a stakeholder map to understand and manage that overall process.

Jim

I probably had an early focus on relationships within the team but I didn't see the full opportunity in that from the start. Opportunities in probably really understanding that stakeholder map and as I am only getting into that now, understanding what are the interactions, how often I should do them, how they will be different with different people.

We probably have a much bigger number, much bigger than I thought. There's a lot of stakeholders in this particular job. Even the amount of stakeholders internally in this part of the business alone: I didn't have a sense of before I went in. It has probably opened my eyes a bit to that and also maybe just pointing me back towards both relationships with those key relationships with my team and not taking any of that for granted.

10

Development

Development was the fourth main theme that emerged, which is about releasing potential within people.

Developing potential and confidence by tapping into inner resources

A number of the leaders mentioned development and the need for more inner workings and what is significant was that a number of leaders questioned their own level of confidence.

John could see the benefit of the inner exploration work that he did with the coach, which opened up new possibilities for him that he experienced as both transformative and exciting.

Paul, Kate and Marion questioned their confidence levels and experienced some inner doubts as they were making the transition from the old to the new. This is important as low levels of confidence and self-belief could lead to a level of stress for the leader and this can have an effect on the team.

Jim

Now that I am six months into the role, I am more confident with what is going on and I don't have to spend more time understanding everything so I can sort through what is the stuff I can let go and what do I need to be more on top of so they are a couple of things.

Kate

I suppose that you can have confidence in the fact that I haven't read everything but I have thought about a couple of salient points that I want to raise here so basically having confidence in the context of shorter time to prepare and be more efficient about how you operate yourself. So very helpful in that regard.

Some of the elements I would struggle with would be you would have a bit of a crisis of confidence from time to time and I can be real candid about it and sometimes when you are in a new role and particularly when you come back from maternity leave. So, I think you can be very 'gung ho' when you are in an interview and you can be very good at selling yourself, but switch off that performance and you go and particularly when you are on mat leave and you come back a year later, you have got to remind yourself of those things. Because she was very good at just reminding me of . . . so I do think it is probably something very sexist to say, I think it is something most women suffer from a lot, in terms of . . . so that's very beneficial in the context of just reminding me of little tools and techniques to remind yourself of what you know and your experience.

John

Facilitating the opening up of possibilities that are your possibilities but you are very unlikely to tap into them or see them yourself. That is what I would see . . . and it is like anything, when someone does something very well, like this lady has done in my own coaching and I think 'Do I do that' could I open up those possibilities with that . . . it's that sort of tapping into your own resources you don't even know you have and those resources creating the possibilities for different things, different areas of development that you didn't necessarily think were there. You weren't aware of, I suppose. It's transformative and it is exciting, for me that is what the a . . . and because you identify them yourself, because they are your possibilities, you sort of go at them that little bit harder than if somebody else suggested them to you.

I was making a transition across to a totally different division but basically no one would really know me and so I felt in that context that really what I could do with is something that could help me tap into my own sort of resources and help me to sort of look at things from a different perspective. What I was really looking towards in the profiles was someone that worked with people who were making transitions.

Paul

You have got to get your own head around your own confidence levels in your role, like that, and I think just feeling ready and able for the role. And for me as I have experience in my role of coaching other people, you know, with the sound of the voice in your head, 'can you really, are you really able for this, can you really do it?' And dealing with that voice in your head was part of it. So, all of those things.

Marion

I think probably one of the things I realized after doing it for the last eight months, I can probably do a lot more of that now with people that I trust well in here and maybe that is part of the confidence piece that has been built over the period.

But I think a big piece was, one of my biggest challenges that I wanted to address was I suppose was building up my own belief in myself and maybe seeing myself as others seem to see me as there may be a bit of a mismatch between those two. So that was a big part of it, building up my confidence I suppose in taking on the role.

Richard

Sorry, I definitely reinforced my beliefs that it wasn't just me that thought I could do these things. This lady is an executive coach talking to me, saying yeah you are well able for these things as well and that kind of reinforced that piece.

She never actually asked what I do day-to-day but just wanted to get an understanding of my motivations, where I see myself going, how I feel about myself in terms of what drives me. All those sorts of things, the inner workings, the subconscious and I found that to be excellent and a bit unnerving initially. It was excellent and I suppose it was a bit like a tap. Once it got turned on, it flew out of me and it gave me a deeper appreciation of what is important. So not necessarily being the smartest in the room or not knowing the most in the room but how to channel all these things together. So, I found it very useful.

To be at your best – meaning, purpose, values

Understanding self and knowing what is important to you as a person are important aspects of one's life.

Paul's approach is viewing his purpose in the broadest sense of life and understanding how that will guide him in his leadership role in the years ahead.

Richard has found through coaching that acceptance of who he is allows him to be at his best to flourish. This is a new and different understanding from what he has received in organizations to date. Richard has also acknowledged aspects of his personality that he needed to be mindful of and he has worked on that, which has also given him positive results.

Paul

I would be better positioned to do what I needed to do as a leader and I was quite open to the whole purpose bit. You know some people maybe struggled a bit with that . . . it's kind of getting into my private life, my work life balance and values and my private life. Now, in fairness to them, they were not trying to act as clinical psychologists. I mean, it wasn't like the psychologist's chair or anything like that but some people might have felt . . . like I was quite open to all that exploration about purpose and meaning. I wasn't over burdened with expectation other than I expected it to be positive. I expected it to help me to explore purpose and meaning and my leadership possibility in the context of my new role. I expected to do that and I expected the unexpected. I wasn't overburdened about pre-conceptions of what it would and wouldn't do.

It did help me crystallize a view of my purpose in its broadest sense of work and life, which is great, and it did help me to explore my leadership possibility and I liked the future focus bit so it was that whole notion of your legacy as you look out three or four years' time and I did all of that very well. I thought that worked well.

Richard

Her main piece was you will get to where you want to get to by getting the most out of yourself or your style and if you try and tailor it and it is nearly like putting a harness on a horse or something, they are not going to be what they could be. So, it is about being authentic. So, you really have to flourish for what you are rather than fit yourself into a box. Which senior leaders if you meet them in organizations, they spend their time telling you to get into a box. That's why I find sometimes that she was totally different.

Source feedback mechanisms for personal stretch and growth

Feedback is a gift. It provides evidence of how others see or experience us. Kate acknowledges feedback that she is now very conscious of. This awareness can bring about new behaviours and create a positive impact for her going forward.

Jim, Helena and John refer to different psychometrics and the benefit of having another perspective as they consider actions they can take for their own personal growth.

Helena

Well there's loads of different tools. Well, one of the things I always find very beneficial anyway is the 360 because that's a real reflection back to you about how people are feeling about you.

Jim

Even just feedback and I guess understanding the psychometrics helped towards pushing me down that road anyway. Especially when I started off in a position where I thought I was a good listener. I thought they knew where I was coming from. I probably did try but I didn't actually act on it. So, I think I can improve on that and I can definitely improve in being a bit more disciplined in how I work as well in that I could be better to let people do the task themselves and stay totally out of it. But I think a certain amount of it will evolve more naturally now that I am six months into the role. I am more confident with what is going on and I don't have to spend more time understanding everything so I can sort through what is the stuff I can let go and what do I need to be more on top of so they are a couple of things. Another thing I would like to do is to be more focused actively building relationships with stakeholders.

And again, I would say before I did the coaching I had good sense that I thought about it but I didn't put it into action half enough and the feedback from the psychometric definitely helped me to say well look, you are not doing that enough, you need to focus more. You might well know, you think you know about it but unless you do it, you are not putting it into action. So, I think that was the core thing I got out of it. I guess as a qualified person coming in during my first two or three years, I was very much focused on tasks and deliverables and deadlines and that was important in the role as well but coaching did it to some extent the first time and it is definitely doing it again this time. It is making me realize the benefit and freeing myself up from the day-to-day to spend a bit of time reflecting and considering things and planning how to engage with people before I do and to see that there is huge merit in that and that is not me taking time out sitting about blue-sky gazing. That is incredibly useful. That gets me the answer from the engagement that we need to progress with whatever aspect of work I want to do.

Kate

So, it's such an obvious question what was your feedback at the last interview and what have you done subsequently and why don't you kind of structure that and there was nothing in that feedback that I found that I disagreed with because it is a very good process. So, we had very good material I think to work with from that perspective.

Another piece of feedback I would have got as well is, in terms of my communication style, and this is something that I have been very conscious of is that not to be too elaborate in my communication and to be conscious of who my audience is. So more internally than externally, I think. I have knocked it on the head because I have been dealing with external regulation for so many years, CEOs and things like that, but more internally in the context of being very conscious of the type of forum I am at, the type of committee structure and what is the point I want to make. That's me elaborating on what my feedback was. So that is what I am saying, I am learning from people.

John

To a degree you could say the psychometrics, the ECR helped a bit with that in terms of my confidence, my straightforwardness. These are the areas that are more confidence related, if we want to call them that. It certainly helped me identify them but also gave me hope that there was a way to improve if I took certain actions or if I . . . self-identified actions that these are things that I could work on and improve. That is really what I got that was very useful out of it.

Identify own authentic leadership approach

Leaders bring their own personal way of being into their role as a leader. What they stand for, their truths and their values.

As a leader Helena sees the need to be a stable presence for her team allowing them their freedom and being there for the team when things become unclear or uncertain.

As a leader Kevin sees the value of the how of leadership now more than ever.

Richard's approach now is to allow himself to show up for who he is instead of shaping himself to fit a certain way. This new approach allows him to be at his best and flourish.

Helena

You know there are different ways of solving things like bringing people together, it's about empowering others, it's about helping you to be a great leader in that context and I think that's where coaching comes into its own. You don't have to do all the things, do you know what I mean? You just have to be the voice of reason when everything else is falling apart and you just have to be, as you say, authentic and you have to be, you know, I suppose clear and you have to be really authentic and you have to bring people with you and you also have to let people have the freedom to be creative and all of those things.

People do look to you, they do, when they get doubts in their head is when you really have to and when the going gets tough, that's when you really have to stay true to yourself.

Kevin

And myself, I was starting to realize that transition piece, even though I said I had been in a leadership role for 20 years. It was all about what you did rather than how you did it. You know, so I was getting more, much more interested in the how, yes, the how.

I said the word light bulb. It totally changed. The light bulb moment for me was the first time I worked with a coach, because it was the first time that I saw that difference between managing and leading. Up to that, even though I had classroom interventions or whatever, but some of those trainings are really text bookie, but through the challenges and the questions and the probings of the coach, it was the first time I really got that click. Yeah, I now really appreciate even though I had done leadership in college but I think it was really that opportunity to say this is about you now and what mark do you want to leave as a leader whereas up to that . . . this is what leadership is generally about and take it or leave it.

Richard

So, it is about being authentic. So, you really have to flourish for what you are rather than fit yourself into a box. Which senior leaders if you meet them in organizations, they spend their time telling you to get into a box. That's why I find sometimes that she was totally different.

Developing others potential – empowerment and autonomy of team

Developing others is a key aspect of leadership that creates a pipeline of talent for the future.

Helena's approach is to create an environment with opportunities for her team to release their potential. She sees that the focus is on her team rather than her.

Helena

It's not about solving everything . . . you know there are different ways of solving things like bringing people together, it's about empowering others, it's about helping you to be a great leader in that context and I think that's where coaching comes into its own. You don't have to do all the things. Do you know what I mean?

I suppose what it created for me was an opportunity to be the best that I can be so that I can actually enjoy creating opportunities for others to be the best that they can be. And I think that actually is that it is not all about the job with me. It's actually about helping others realize their potential and to create the environment for them to shine. And I think that for me and coaching actually helped me to realize that about myself. And I might have missed that completely.

Kevin

If I never read another book about leadership that was sort of one of the things I took away from it. Absolutely, no one is not talent today. The question is what is their appetite and ambition? But also, a little bit of a lift up . . . if you can raise everybody up and others grow on the back of others. It causes a momentum or like a snowball going down the hill and it suddenly becomes massive.

John

I am reasonably relaxed with myself so because of that then I am quite comfortable then sharing my strengths but also my development points with people around me and being open and just establishing that level of trust, basically to be able to develop good teams, to develop good leaders too. One way I would call myself is like a multiplier so that I can develop good teams and develop good people.

Letting go and delegating

Letting go of the expert mindset is important as people move into leadership roles. Learning to let go and delegate is an important aspect of the new behaviour required.

Kate and Richard give an understanding of how moving from being the expert to learning to delegate is a key aspect of their new way of being as a leader.

Jim

And I have ambitions to be a more senior leader and if the likes of manager X as finance director and other directors, they don't deliver themselves, they deliver through people.

Kate

Because you are the subject matter expert in all of that kind of stuff. Trusting your team, you know. So, I found her very, very helpful in the context of just kind of, as you become more senior in the organization, how you stop doing the things you had done before because otherwise if you keep doing those, you are still operating at the same level and you are not growing and making sure you are really operating at the right level.

Richard

And the other one which is very important is focussing on the knitting, getting the three to five things and focus on them and get rid of the noise. So, I delegate like hell and I challenge what I should and shouldn't be part of and what I add value to and you can get recognition for and all these sorts of things. So, one learning is what you do.

I delegated a bit more but as a consequence of this. I found myself less busy because I would have always been the one previously to get down to the detail and make sure that I knew as much as everyone else and I do well to fill up eight hours now.

Gain new insights (light bulb moments)

New awareness and new ways of seeing opens our eyes to new possibilities, which creates new futures. This is important for leaders who need to build their repertoire for innovation and creativity.

Through reflection, Jim's deeper awareness of the value of relationships is coming more to the fore, which creates more meaning for him. He acknowledges that this awareness is intuitive as much as cognitive, so he is tapping into more aspects of himself. This will lead to adjustments in his behaviour that will create the results he is looking for.

John indicates that the coach's facilitation of a board simulation exercise allowed more deeper exploration for him. By taking a helicopter view of the setting and looking at the overall piece from different angles, it allowed him to see more opportunities and possibilities.

Helena

I suppose this is one of the things where coaching helped me . . . you know, erm I suppose all my life I have always been a very driven person and, you know, delivering results would have been very important to me and erm I suppose I am very hard on myself and I suppose what coaching made me appreciate was the talents I could bring to the table as well and how you can bring people with you. So, I suppose one of my strengths that I discovered or a by-product which I really didn't think I had before was the strong leadership skills that I have, the ability I have to create the environment for people, in a psychological safe environment where people can speak openly, where we can plan together and there is no such thing as a wrong suggestion.

But also setting out the long-term vision and creating that vision for people and getting the energy or having or bringing the energy I should say, that people get excited and enthused about getting on the bus with you and then I suppose and it's not something I ever realized I did or that I do quite naturally because, you know, when I take on a role or whatever, I just take it on. I see the challenges that there are and I also see the opportunities and I talk in a language of opportunity and motivation rather than challenge and issues because you know they are all there, of course they are, but behind every challenge is an opportunity and it is about creating that kind of space for people to feel, yes, gosh yes, somebody has our back, oh yes, I can make that suggestion. That they lose their fear and therefore the skills and the talent they have, you really unleash them. And creating that enthusiasm and energy.

Like, yes, of course I am a good organizer and a good worker and yes all of those good things that you would expect but it is that kind of, what I see as and I haven't seen before, is that I do see the big picture and I can stand up and I am not afraid to say I don't have all the answers. I need help here, you are my team, do you know what I mean? You create that environment that everybody wants to be a part of and get quite excited about it and I get quite excited, thrilled.

Jim

Self-awareness, mostly of myself, but also of other people and the things like listening and empathy that all come from that relationship but the thing about where if someone wants to work with you, you will get somewhere faster and better and understanding where they are and where you are. To me, that all wraps into and just as I am speaking, it is coming to me that awareness of self and that awareness of the other person probably and that idea of purpose and direction and values. All that intangible that isn't, let's say, at the front of our brain. It does more of that gut and sleeping on it. That is coming out for me more, which I am delighted about.

John

The last coaching session we had, I mean, I do coaching internally now but what she did, she got me into a sort of a . . . using figures and bits of things and asking where are you and where is everybody else and where do you want them to be. You know, it was sort of very conceptual but it was very . . . I found it was huge, it brought up so many different opportunities or possibilities and I think that is the value of it. It wasn't that the possibilities came from her, it was facilitated by her but it came from me. That is what the value was. I actually walked in from a location after it which is about five miles or something like that and I felt great after it. I felt I needed the walk just to think out all these things, these opportunities and possibilities that were going through my head, following it.

Certainly, the way this was done, more emerged perhaps rather than from a conversation because it is different . . . it was just those kind of questions, where are you in relation to this group and it is natural in terms of . . . but if someone had said to me think about this. It was just . . . I wouldn't have been able to match that.

Career – managing from here to the future

Career means different things to different people. In organizational life it is generally understood as moving laterally or being promoted vertically to a more senior position. Jim sees career in stages that relate to his age and this transition has now signalled another stage. Jim in his interview referred to the air getting thinner as you reach the top and he is already considering what the next stage could be for him.

Richard acknowledges his brashness could have held him back in his careering going forward. He gives some credit to coaching for feedback and in preparing him to get the opportunity to be a part of the senior leadership team.

Jim

How is this going to pan out now that I am in my mid-30s compared to when I was in my 20s I was going to plan out where I am going to be in the next five or six years . . . where am I going to be at the end of it. So, there are bigger strategic questions if you like around career as well. So that made it a bit harder to put a picture on what I want exactly out of the coaching.

Richard

I had been brought onto the senior leadership group in Company X and I think I may have been considered before but I kind of reined in my brashness a bit and I think I wouldn't have got that opportunity if I had been as brash as I originally had been. So yeah, it probably wouldn't have happened but it was a result of it [the coaching].

On that point, one thing I think is very important and it is that it's the difference between someone who thinks they are helping you in your career but isn't doing you much good and this sort of coaching.

Sustainable learning – action learning in role and transferrable application of tools and techniques

When new learning is applied in real-life scenarios, the impact is visible and this can be transformative as the person's belief in their ability raises. New techniques can also be found to be useful when applied to different scenarios.

Jim and Kate acknowledge new tools that have been valuable to them in dealing with issues.

Jim

Back in 2013 after my first promotion to a senior manager and I wasn't successful I went and got that book and picked up through some of the process that empathy and engaging people is something I could practise more even If I understood it. And when I thought I was being empathetic, maybe I wasn't bringing it into action with my team and that is something I focused on quite a bit. So that emotional capital side . . .

I could see the picture that I wanted and I absolutely got there and I even did it a bit better and I learnt lots of . . . quite a bit along the way about personalities in the team that I was managing and I engaged with them and I felt that they had grown with me as I had kind of used these tools so that gave me a real sense of the value of coaching.

Kate

Yes, just some small tools made a significant difference in terms of, as I said, meeting preparation and things like that and I take copious notes when I am at these sessions and just as a frame of reference so I would get articles from her as well and she would send me on things I could think about so just remind yourself in terms of your interactions.

It might have taken longer so I think she could have short circuited some of the issues I was grappling with myself so in a way that gave me tools that I wouldn't have been aware of.

Well, in the first instance it has had the desired effect in terms of a promotional opportunity so I would like to think that I am behaving differently because I am taking some of the things that we are discussing. I think it's one of those things that you have to keep reminding yourself. I think that, like one of my downfalls is I go to training sessions and I don't apply, like some people are very good and very disciplined about applying stuff afterwards and I find it really beneficial and I must remember that and I look back and my notes are fantastic and I am not . . . kind of.

Yes, in certain circumstances I am applying stuff but I am still learning. It's not like I have got my feedback, I have been promoted and now I need to stop doing those things. I need to continue, continue, continue.

Kevin

The following coaching sessions focused on re-affirming the good, so not to lose those and mostly about the stops. I suppose the rest of the coaching was about how we can grow.

11 Leadership Transition Coaching questions

Four themes were identified from the research. They are *Time to think, Clarity and focus, Collaborate with others* and *Development.* A number of subordinate themes were generated under each of the four main themes.

Additionally, to add to the framework, questions have been included as an aid for the reader to reflect on the areas that are relevant at times of transition.

Leadership Transition Coaching Framework

(Note: the questions below were adapted after the research was carried out. They may be helpful to consider as prompts only for your own thinking. It is not intended that they be prescriptive questions as the client's agenda and the unique context remains at the forefront of the coaching engagement).

Themes and subordinate themes

Main theme	Subordinate theme
Time to think	**Finding your feet in a new dynamic**
	What is uniquely new and different about this new role?
	What are some of the dynamics that you are becoming aware of?
	Who are the key stakeholders and influencers in these dynamics?
	What are some of the things you need to think about as you navigate forward?
	How can you navigate the journey to the new normal?
	Discipline of reflecting to create value in a very busy world
	What could be a valuable takeaway from your time spent in coaching?

In your first 100 days, what quick wins could add value for you?

In a year's time from now, what will you regret not having addressed today?

Have thinking and assumptions challenged.

Will it add value to be challenged by your coach?

What assumptions could you be making about this role?

How is this role challenging your capabilities and skills?

Create space to think and plan to develop vision and direction

How can you strategically plan for you and your team?

What do you require in order to create a clear vision?

How will you provide sufficient support and clarity to achieve the vision?

Widen the lens with critical thinking to explore challenges and opportunities

What opportunities might there be that you are now becoming aware of?

What are some challenges you might face?

What might other leaders in your position do in this situation?

How comfortable are you working in the unknown?

How is the role shaping your thinking?

Clarity and focus

A psychologically safe environment with trust and openness

Will you highlight when you do not feel supported or challenged enough?

What might you be holding back?

On a rating of 1 to 10, how comfortable are you with this approach?

Download and get structure on the issues

Where are you now in your understanding of the role?

What are the big issues you will need to deal with in this role?

How much control or influence do you have around this issue?

Broaden perspective by developing a wider lens

What other options might you have?

What is the worst-case scenario?

If you knew you could deal with this, what would that look like?

Operate at the right level for impact and influence

Who do you need to influence and how do you go about connecting with them?

How do you know you are having the right kind of impact?

How do you measure the impact you have in your role?

Have you received any relevant feedback?

Can you think of a senior leader who is a good role model for you?

Gain clarity and focus on priorities and develop a plan

How clear are you on what you are being commissioned to deliver in the context of all of your stakeholders (e.g. board, investors, customers, employees, communities, regulators, government bodies, partner organizations)?

What are key areas that are important for you to focus on?

What is the single greatest thing that will affect the greatest amount of change right now?

What will you have that you don't have right now?

Knowing what you know now, what specifically do you now want to do about X?

What would a plan look like for you?

Check-in to review and revise

What has been happening for you and your team?

Can I check in with you with regards to where we left off on our last conversation?

How have you been adapting in the role?

Has anything happened in the meantime that you were not expecting (either good or otherwise)?

What might be useful to concentrate on at this session?

Working smart and sustaining focus and energy

How are your energy levels?

What drains your energy? How do you recover?

In terms of managing your own resources, are there things you could do differently if you allowed yourself?

How do you protect your energy and build resilience?

Collaborate with others	**Collaborate with new leadership team (leader of leaders) to develop one vision**

How can you best collaborate with your direct reports to develop alignment?

What do you need your leaders to deliver on in order to align with the vision?

Flex approach for effective interactions and engagement with different personalities

How comfortable are you in dealing with the diversity of personalities across your team and with your stakeholders?

How can you best prepare for impactful communication across different audiences?

How can you best get to know and understand your direct reports?

How do you build and sustain effective relationships?

Navigate the journey with the team and bring them on board

How best can you share your plans for moving forward with your team?

What do you need to do to engage your team and build followership?

Are there key aspects of the current culture that you need to consider and why?

What change might you need to bring about in the current context?

Setting expectations and performance conversations

What do clear and engaging performance conversations look like?

How can you best prepare to have effective and engaging performance conversations?

Have key deliverables and performance indicators been identified?

Is there any further information that you will need to gather before holding the conversations?

Will review meetings be scheduled to take place and how often?

Have you experienced any mechanism that works best around reviewing progress on key deliverables?

Build new relationships and networks

What new relationships and networks might you need to pay attention to?

How comfortable are you in initiating the building of new relationships?

Are there new networks you will need to link in with?

What approach do you need to develop to effectively engage with new stakeholders?

Identify a stakeholder plan early

Have you thought about mapping out the key stakeholders you will need to engage with (both those internally within the organization and externally)?

What type of engagements will you have with each of these stakeholders?

Are there any opportunities or risks associated with these relationships?

How can you best prepare for and prioritize interactions with the potential list of stakeholders?

What might be a key value for you in engaging with stakeholders early?

Development

Developing potential and confidence by tapping into inner resources

On a scale of 1 to 10 how confident are you about taking on this role?

What are you looking forward to as you take on this new leadership role?

What might get in the way of you showing up at your best as a leader?

Who could be a sounding board for you in your network?

To be at your best – meaning, purpose and values

Tell me about the significance of this role.

What does this role personally mean for you?

How do you aspire to making an impact in this role? In this organization?

Have you considered your own personal values and what you bring to this role?

How might your values get compromised and how will you handle that?

What would you like your legacy to be in this role?

Source feedback mechanisms for personal stretch and growth

Have you received feedback after the interview or through a development process recently?

Have you received any informal feedback since coming into the new role?

Do you know what your strengths are? Impact of overplaying them?

What might be helpful for you to stop, start, continue doing?

On a rating of 1 to 10, how aware are you of your emotional intelligence?

What is the likely impact of your emotions on your thoughts and behaviour?

What is the value of tuning into the emotions of others?

Identify own authentic leadership approach

Who do you want to be as a leader?

What do you want to be known for?

Can you think of a leader that has left a positive impression on you and why?

What are you like when you are at your best?

How do you show up as a leader?

What will you want to be remembered for by your team and peers?

Develop others' potential – empowerment and autonomy of team

What kind of working environment do you want to foster?

What are the top three things you want to foster in your team?

How will you build trust within your team?

How will you know when you have gained the trust of your team?

How can you best ensure you develop your team and get the best outcome for everyone?

Letting go and delegating

What might you need to let go of?

What worked well for you in the past but may not be needed so much going forward?

What is the key difference in how you now need to operate day to day?

How can you prepare for this change?

What is the value of delegating?

How will you know you are operating at the right level?

Gain new insights (light bulb moments)

Is there anything new that has emerged that you were not expecting?

Are there any new things that you have learned along the way?

What have you keenly become aware of?

Is there anything that has surprised you?

Career – manging from here to the future

What are your thoughts on what career means for you?

Do you have a picture of what your career might look like three to five years from now?

What opportunities might this role open up for you in the future?

How long do you see yourself being in this role?

Sustainable learning – action learning in role and transferrable application of tools and techniques

Are there any specific learnings you can take away from the coaching sessions and use?

If you knew what to do in a situation, what might hold you back from actioning it?

What would be one key growth area that you have identified for yourself?

Are there any tools that you have applied that have made a difference?

If there was one further technique, tool or support that would benefit you in your role, what might that be?

Note: A reminder that these questions were adapted after the research was carried out and are intended only as prompts. It is not intended that they be prescriptive questions but can be a roadmap for your thinking at this time of transition. As always, the client's agenda and their unique context remains at the forefront of the coaching engagement.

12 Case studies

Beyond the eight leaders who participated in the research for the thesis, more recently four further leaders were interviewed about their experience of transitioning to a new leadership role and their experience of transitioning is outlined below.

Case study 1 – transitioning to a more senior role can be daunting

Kim worked for a pharmaceutical company and was approached about joining the senior team in a new role of overall office manager. Up to this point, Kim was the office co-ordinator across all the business functions, from Finance to IT and more. Kim was very apprehensive about taking on this new promotional position. It meant she would be removing herself from the work that she felt she was comfortable with and she enjoyed her work with the team that reported to her. She was resistant to taking on the new more senior role and her senior manager offered her coaching in order to take some time out to reflect before making a final decision to accept or decline the new role.

Kim was willing to engage with a coach on the basis that the final decision would be her own. She engaged with a coach for six sessions over a three-month period and through the process was able to start clarifying her thoughts and concerns, getting insight to her beliefs and how that coloured her thinking and also understanding what her values were. During this time, she started sitting in on senior management meetings to gain insight into the more strategic business agenda. She started to consider the development of the team she had managed and started to delegate more responsibility to those team members. Her confidence level and career aspirations were areas she grappled with but over time she got clarity from the exercises she undertook with the coach and the reflective questions and other conversations she had with her senior manager, which took place between her coaching sessions.

By the end of the coaching sessions, Kim had developed a way forward for other questions regarding the future of her work and a tentative future work location change she aspired to but had never articulated to management before.

The tools that were used during the coaching sessions included a wheel on which the coach asked Kim to map out areas of responsibility within the role she was currently undertaking. From that Kim considered priorities and areas where she could delegate. During the coaching sessions, a strengths assessment and a leadership EQi2.0 assessment were undertaken, both being self-assessments. Additionally, Kim also got an opportunity to explore her values.

The coach had a three-way meeting with Kim (client) and the CEO (sponsor) prior to the coaching commencing and also at completion stage.

Note the coaching tools mentioned are being referenced only as potential tools that were selected by the coach in that given situation. Note that another coach may have taken a different approach and while these tools were very helpful, be mindful that a one size does not fit all.

Each coach and leader will have their own style and preferences for how they want to engage.

Case study 2 – transitioning from specialist to leader

David started out in his career ten years ago in 2010 having achieved an arts qualification. At this time the world was experiencing a deep economic recession, which brought with it an employment freeze in many organizations and while David enjoyed his work, he just about managed to obtain some short work assignments from time to time. He decided to take on a master's programme, which brought him into the world of business media. He later undertook studies in the field of digital communications, which has enhanced his capability and allowed him to become a specialist in his field of work.

Over the past ten years, he has held five roles and he feels he has learned much over those assignments, which have been mainly project based roles. In the past year he took a move, as a specialist, from one of the big four consultancy firms to a global company, which gives him international experience. He was in this new role five months when his senior leader was promoted to director and David was approached about taking on a leadership role where he would have four communication specialists reporting to him and all working virtually in different global locations. So he has experienced much change during this time.

I met David just after he was appointed to the Global Communications Manager role at a time when the global health pandemic of COVID-19 was happening. He describes three to four months of an informal transition period when he was going through the selection process for the manager role and even though he had not yet been appointed, as the selection process was still underway, it gave him time to understand who the key stakeholders were, understand their remit and also understand the makeup of the team. He had little information to go on so he started by focusing on the key objectives for the organization, both on a global level and also understanding the different aspects of each location within the organization.

Following his appointment to the role in March 2020, business priorities quickly escalated to respond to the COVID-19 pandemic. David acknowledges that the company structure was different to what he experienced before and it felt unfamiliar to him as he was working now in what he describes as a very niche area. He was also experiencing the pressure coming from leadership at HQ in terms of what this function needed to achieve in terms of business as usual and later the impact of COVID-19 pandemic on work. David describes below his transition to date.

So, in terms of the volume of learning that was required, it was critical to break down and understand the key priorities that I needed to know and I suppose, park everything else. And then on top of all of that, I also needed to understand how best to structure information to match my own style. And that was basically created by approaching one-to-one sessions with each of the key stakeholders to understand what they wanted to achieve, who their key stakeholders were and to understand what their challenges and opportunities were at a local level.

From a human point of view, it was quite exhausting. Even though I had a team of two direct reports (and carried a further two specialist roles which would not now be filled due to a recruitment freeze) along with other people I relied on to deliver in their own business functions. In terms of managing, basically I have to work on what the key priorities are, park everything else that isn't a priority. And if it is a priority, it will be called up in a meeting or a follow-up email in terms of something that can't be parked. It needs to be prioritized. So you are constantly juggling, constantly reviewing priorities. And each time a situation changes globally, for example a lockdown in India for 21 days, you have to keep re-prioritizing the whole time to understand in real time what the business is trying to achieve and the challenges globally for that. So it demands a lot of energy and a lot of thinking power.

Well, to maintain the performance, the first thing you do is to delegate to the team that you do have. So even if it's two out of four, it is better to keep those sites covered as they have local knowledge and an understanding of local nuance so they were able to manage that. So rather than delegate and tell them what to do, I was checking in to see were they OK and to identify what do they need, so I was coaching them. And then asking questions for understanding and clarity. I had undertaken coaching as part of my previous training and I am comfortable with that approach and I have also experienced coaching in a project capacity in the past.

For this transition, I did work with a coach as I felt I was transitioning into this new role as manager as it was a step change from the specialist roles I have come from and I sourced a coach I had known. First of all, it allows time to think. So when I am working in crisis mode there isn't an opportunity to think in a broader sense. Time doesn't allow it. And it also enables the person to detach from the information in fight or flight mode and understand the information from other perspectives rather than on the one deliverable they have to achieve. And it also gives an opportunity to understand the big picture in terms of what's next. So it gives them the opportunity to think strategically. It also manages their energy.

Rather than draining the adrenaline system by constantly reacting, the person starts pre-empting and starts understanding what the key themes and trends are. And I suppose using energy to keep the work progressing but also not over-exerting themselves to manage their own velocity but also that of the team. Because the leader sets the tone for the team so it is important that I can maintain that. It is also a safe space. Because in the organization, voicing concerns or raising questions is not welcomed and depends on culture and the style of leadership. Again, it is a safe space for people to be able to ask questions or voice an opinion especially when a manager is on their own and there is no second opinion.

Choice of culture and leadership that you work with becomes quite apparent when you take on a manager role, because the management is the middle bit between the senior leadership and the employees, as well as being the key diplomat for other teams. They are the person that connects with other functions outside of their team and it is the leadership team that either supports that or, I suppose, makes it more difficult. So depending on the support and the direction given by senior leaders, that basically sets the tone for how that manager can operate. So although the manager has autonomy, he has to work within the culture and expectations of leadership, who ultimately determine his performance over the year.

Adaptability to different styles is important. In addition to understanding ways of working and style. It is also understanding how different people process and perceive the situation. So in addition to changing your working style, whatever the technical aspects of that might be. Also understanding the different personalities that are driving how a team functions. A team that functions in one organization might function differently in another and that can influence everything in the way they structure and collaborate, to how they discuss and engage at a very basic level.

Case study 3 – leadership transition to director

Jane, an ex-director of a public sector organization, having completed a coaching qualification became an associate in a coaching partnership. She coaches executives who have either been promoted or are currently in positions at C suite level (directors and CEOs). Here, she reflects on a client whom she coached as the client was transitioning into a new role as director in a multi-national organization. Below provides a lens into the coach's perspective of that experience.

I suppose it is very individual and depending on where people are coming from. But what I am really seeing is the sense of being alone. An understanding that you are moving from a very collective kind of thing to a lonely spot. And what I am seeing with people is that transition to being that one person where the buck stops with you. And what I see particularly is, people have a good understanding of the requirements of the role, for example the role and the responsibility. But where I am seeing people struggle a little bit is the whole sense of what that means at an individual level and being ready in a way to be the one where the buck stops with you.

It is not about managing anymore. It is that switch from being the manager to the leader and it is really kind of letting go an awful lot as well of what you previously thought you knew and thought was important. And I think there is a significant piece of saying to people you have got to let go of the stuff that made you successful up to now and now you are getting into a space where, OK, you know, some of the stuff that made you what you are is no longer required. And it is that sense of that is no longer going to be your hallmark for success. You know, you were a brilliant technician, analyst or whatever, you were a brilliant people manager, because this even means you have to stop managing. And the things that you were good maybe at doing, especially around managing people, isn't even what's required now. It's that further step up again.

It's that piece of actually letting people be what they are being but kind of guide them as opposed to manage them. And I think that is a bit scary for people and they say 'what do you mean'. And you as coach say 'you are brilliant with people and all that like and you still need to be brilliant with people but you are not going to be their manager. You are going to be their leader.' So you are more like making sure they are allowed to grow, develop and you have got to delegate and watch them grow as such. But it's just letting things go and the other thing I think a lot of people struggle with, too, is that whole strategic piece as well. A lot of people come out of operational type roles and then struggle a bit when it comes to the more strategic piece that they are asked to be looking forward and big thinking. And I think some people struggle with that a little bit as well. So it is about that kind of making sure that they have that strategic focus as opposed to getting down into the operational details and all of that.

I think there is a sense that people feel what made me successful will always kind of keep me successful. And you are sort of saying 'No, you were successful up to now because that was what was required of you up to now. But that is not what will make you successful. The next piece required is for you to be slightly different from how you have always been and there is that sense of 'I don't want to let this go because it is where I am comfortable and all of that'. So there is a bit of the loneliness about being on your own and the buck stopping with you. And having that kind of capability to stand back and make those calls and make those decisions. And maybe a bit about the individual where that is required.

In your experience then, while coaching somebody in that space, how long does it generally take for them to come through and to find their wings as such and find that they are moving across?

Quite honestly, I think it is a year. I am thinking of one person in particular I have been working with and I am thinking we had 2 × 6 month programmes.

The first programme was quite intensive coaching and the second one was more mentoring. I could definitely see a change. There was a huge amount of coaching and kind of spending an awful lot of time making sure that you were challenging them and putting the onus back on them. And then in the second six months I could see where you were much more kind of listening to what they were planning to do and finding that there was very little where you were saying and 'what would you do and why'. You could even see their confidence growing. But I still think you almost needed the two phases for them. It was like, in the beginning, you were very much their coach and very much trying to ensure they were developing and pushing it back to them. Whereas in the second phase, you were more their sounding board. And that particular guy was an interesting one.

And at the end he wanted to re-new again. And I was saying 'I actually don't think you need to'. But I didn't want him to become too dependent either. But I definitely saw that shift and I was looking back on my notes when we were finished and I could see I had far less notes for the second phase. And for the second phase it was much more him talking, but talking through things but it was coming from himself. Whereas at first there was a lot of silences, there was a lot of me saying 'why would you do that'. Whereas the second one was him coming forward with much more content and at times I would say 'what are you thinking about that' but it was much more definitely mentoring in the second phase of it.

Case study 4 – transitioning to board level

Stephanie is a board member of three organizations representing large public and private enterprises. More recently she has become a chair on the board of a national government regulatory body. While she has not been coached in transition to these roles, she has shared her experience and thoughts on both joining boards and becoming chair of a board and discusses how she sees that coaching can have a role to play at that time of transition.

There is more and more responsibility being landed on boards in terms of governance and it can often be quite a difficult spot for chairs to find themselves in, particularly, and I think the big one is the relationship between the chair and the CEO. And I think that for individual board members as well, I think their relationship with the executive and with the CEO as well. And oftentimes, I think there is a misalignment, a misunderstanding and often a significant amount of tension. And I think there is a huge emphasis on, in coaching particularly, around the executive and coaching for performance and all that, and equally there has to be the same, if you like, support for boards as well as them and coaching them for their performance because an awful lot of boards, I think, are not performing the way they should be performing.

I don't think they fully understand their brief and I think they have responsibility that an awful lot of the time isn't clearly understood and when it is understood they are very unclear as to how they personally execute that responsibility. So it is certainly an area, I think, that requires a huge amount of attention and there is some training in that going in there. But the training is kind of around your responsibilities and it is quite legalistic in terms of pointing out what the role holder is responsible for.

Where there is a big gap is, I think, is how the board should behave and how it should equally both challenge and support. And I think an awful lot of people find that, if you like, almost, they are like two opposite types of kind of relationships. But I think an awful lot of people find it difficult to understand what that means for them at an individual level. And they don't fully understand what it means. I think some of them are quite comfortable in challenge. An awful lot of them think support is just saying nothing. I have been on a number of boards where, quite honestly, people have just nodded their heads, like, and it is unclear then whether that is support or not or what it all amounts to. So it's a challenge but I think there is definitely opportunities there for coaching and there should be far more coaching in there.

With the larger organizations, while the responsibility might be greater, you find that they are more formalized, that they have more procedures and all of that. You could be talking about different types of issues but I do think the inherent thing of being that CEO, having to let go. I do think you find the same. What you might find in the larger organizations is a little bit more of the internal stakeholder management coming to the fore. But you do find in smaller organizations the things that are a bit more . . . obviously a lot of relationship coaching goes on. There are difficult relationships with reportees' boards, I am finding with CEOs . . . but a couple of them, and I have seen it myself and even in my own, tension between the board and the chair and the CEO. And one of the things which I have noticed, which is an interesting thing is I found . . . one board that I am on now . . . the guy who is chairing it was also a CEO himself and he is not long retired as a CEO. And I can see the struggle that he has. He thinks he is CEO still and he acts and thinks like one still.

He has not made that transition from being the CEO. He thinks he has and the difficulty in their relationship now is that he is thinking like the CEO and she is trying to be the CEO and they are clashing.

Clearly, transitioning into a role as any new role really, but it is more particular where you have significant roles like chairs of boards and CEOs that people recognize that they have to actually make a transition. And I think people think, well, I was a very successful CEO and so now I will be a very successful chair without realizing that there is a transition to be made.

And, equally, that you do find people in organizations and they say 'I have been appointed CEO' as a new job and they will recognize they have a new job with new responsibilities and all that, but, not recognize there is a transition to be made from how they have operated. How they think and even how they interact with others. That is where it is important as well at board level but particularly for chairs and collectively for a board to understand that for, whatever reason, they have been selected that they now have to transition to be a board member for that organization. They have to understand the purpose of that organization but also how they interact with the other directors that are appointed and how collectively they can work together for that organization.

And you have to assume and we should be able to assume that all the right technical and legal stuff is done. But it is beyond that then, like, what is the quality of the kind of decisions we are making. Are they strategic enough? That is another thing . . . I find an awful lot of boards start dabbling into the operations of the business. They don't feel comfortable in the strategic space, which is really where they need to be. And there is the element of this is the space we need to be in, really working together in this kind of space and then collectively how well are we working together to really make sure we really are making this a better organization. We are not just simply ticking along but it's that bit where coaching could really come on to say there is a good cohesive team here that work here together.

I think it does come back to your purpose and why you are here and as a team, the collective responsibility that you have as a team to do that. And again, it's that space that requires us . . . because people are coming from very busy lives and their full-time jobs somewhere else. They are coming in and it is just another meeting. I think that it is not just another meeting. It is to get that understanding is . . . it isn't just another meeting. You are here because there is a purpose to what this organization is doing and you as a team are part of that purpose and you have a role to play in advancing that purpose.

And I think the risk is that . . . I am here now and it is another meeting. The papers are grand and move onto the next item.

13 Evidence-based journey through transition

In a CIPD (2014) research report, insights on the evolving nature of leadership were provided based on over 120 interviews and focus groups with managers, employees and HR practitioners in seven large organizations. They observed from their study that the need for leadership has changed following the global shifts in the ways we work today. This report signals a need to consider focusing efforts on understanding what leadership the specific organization needs and whether the leadership approach is aligned to the organizational context.

Their report notes that while organizations are seen to be better at understanding leadership at the highest levels in the hierarchy, many are now seeking to devolve leadership down the line, expecting more junior managers and employees without managerial responsibility to treat the organizational agenda as their own. This also signals that transitions are not solely based on promotion but can be lateral moves, project based, change through mergers, re-structuring and more.

The underpinning value or principle in exploring our research on the impact of coaching on leaders in transition is that it seeks to be meaningful to organizations as they consider strategies to support leadership transitions in organizational life, which have become more challenged with increasingly difficult and more complex competitive demands and to individuals in their everyday working or personal lives.

The findings can offer real value by identifying key aspects that the leaders identify as having had significant impact for them. It is the researchers' view that exploring the impact of coaching on leaders as they transition to a new role in the workplace can be of benefit to both organizations and individuals. In particular, the HR profession such as organizational development managers, HR managers, learning and development managers, leaders, coaches and coaching bodies may consider these findings in the context of a potential for development solutions for leaders.

Personalized coaching is probably more effective for preventing derailment than leadership development training programmes because such programmes focus on training leadership and business skills (Burke and Day 1986; Csoka 1997) rather than the interpersonal and intrapersonal deficits at the root of derailment (Kaiser and Kaplan 2006). A coach can offer a supportive and trusting relationship that can call out thoughts, beliefs and assumptions that need to be discussed. The findings suggest that coaching creates a unique dynamic that brings multiple positive experiences, including the opportunity to consider perspectives, view options, consider opportunities and sustain focus and resilience as the leader makes the transition into a new role.

The research findings suggest coaching has a significant impact in many aspects for the new leaders. Each leader brings their own unique experience and sense-making to their experience of coaching at that time of transition. Each leader exhibited individual differences and emphasis on different aspects of coaching, illustrating there is no one-size-fits-all approach.

The overall findings extensively cover all key aspects that were found through interviews with the leaders. However, there was a definite consensus among the leaders on specific aspects of the impact of coaching.

The first aspect is that coaching offers a unique trusting space for the leader to bring themselves fully into the room. This is seen as the most critical ingredient to the value that is to be derived from the coaching relationship. That trust is a key aspect of bond and engagement. With the ever-accelerating pace of organizational life with constant change in both internal and external environments, organizational politics and business as usual to be carried out, there was a strong consensus that coaching brings a unique place to land as the leader navigates their way forward.

The second aspect where there was consensus from the leaders was around people and getting the best out of those relationships.

The third aspect of consensus was around self-awareness and their own leadership approach. The leader was able to apply learning in action and was being exposed to new ways of thinking and new techniques. Coaching meetings allowed a check-in with a look back and look forward approach. This type of sustainable learning and the transferability of the new learning and techniques brings added value to the leaders.

A keen observation would have been the resilience that is needed to sustain the level of performance by the new leader. The realization by the leaders that the delivery of work will be primarily carried out by others is a significant change for new leaders who have understood that their technical expertise has brought them success so far and that is what they were rewarded for in the past. Letting go and delegating is a key aspect of the bridge that needs to be crossed for many new leaders. Even the most senior of leaders can have blind spots and make assumptions about what is required when they move to a new role (see Case study 4: transitioning to board level, p. 137).

Some of the leaders experienced a dip in confidence even when they had been in leadership roles for many years. The move to a more senior level and to a new role within a new landscape can bring with it dormant triggers of self-doubt around their capability. New levels of unknowing and uncertainty when met with expressed great expectations from others can bring new insecure emotions to the fore, which can over time lead to anxiety. This is where the leader's level of self-awareness and self-regulation become part of the inner resources that they can tap into in order to sustain their inner self-belief and clarity of mind.

Two interesting observations came through the research. The first one was that a leader could cognitively know what they needed to do in a situation so they had the awareness and thought they were showing up in a positive light, yet through feedback they realized it was not having the desired effect. This reinforces the value of feedback from others, which is also a part of the coaching process and is often where new insights and self-awareness and growth happens. The second observation was the ambitious nature of a leader and the pace with which the new leader was expending energy on moving to the next senior role of director having just arrived in the current new role. While it is admirable, expectations are high and the number of positions at that level in the organization would be small, so how will they sustain their meaning and purpose in the new role?

In the area of leadership development, Passmore (2010) argues that coaching can contribute in a number of ways. They include helping leaders to transfer learning and making links from theory to practice and from conceptual to previous knowledge. A second benefit is to enhance skills and a third area is in the development of greater self-awareness. A fourth potential benefit of leadership coaching is through enhancing the motivation of leaders. A fifth area where coaching can demonstrate a positive contribution in leaders is in helping them develop stronger personal confidence or self-regard (Evers, Brouwers and Tomic 2006). The final area where coaching can impact on leadership is through well-being. The bottom-line requirement for post-modern organizations, companies and communities is that leadership be a coachable skill (Wood and Gordon 2009).

Overall, the findings align with research that has been carried out to date. The four themes and their subordinate themes can offer a lens that can be useful for relevant stakeholders to consider if they are making transitions or if they are supporting other leaders while making a transition to a new role.

A clear message that echoed through the interviews with the leaders was that they have a strong desire to build collaborative relationships with their team and their stakeholders as they know that their results, which are the organization's results, will primarily come through others. Depending on the business context of the organization, one size does not fit all for leaders in terms of the support they may need.

In today's world the importance for a leader to coach those they work with is now widely recognized. A leader who takes a coaching approach (where appropriate) takes conversations and engagement to another level. The attention within those conversations promotes clear thinking that works towards clarity of expectations, exploring options and an agreed way forward. So instead of 'Do as I say', the dialogue opens up a conversation whereby the other person becomes a thinking partner and the process is more engaging and allows more autonomy. I heard this phrase some years ago and it made a lot of sense 'he/she who creates the solution owns the solution'. From the leader's perspective, a coaching approach (GROW model is often used) can be an effective way to build relationships, engage with others and set people up for success. As much as the way to have a coaching conversation is considered, how to have that conversation is also important. Listening skills and questioning are inherent and an understanding of the role of emotional intelligence can be beneficial.

Equally, with so much of a draw on people's attention in today's fast paced environment, whether inside or outside of work, the presence of the leader and their ability to sustain their own and the team's performance and resilience will be a measure of their own success.

Much has been written about talent acquisition and talent management over recent years and leaders to new positions are that talent. With so much time and cost invested in the resourcing of the new leader and so much expectation around their anticipated arrival, maybe it is worth considering what is the best way to support the leader as they transition to a new role whether that is an in-house or external solution. Investment in coaching can accelerate the new leader's effectiveness and shows that the company cares along with reducing the chance of an early departure, which can carry significant cost. The key consideration in all of this, is how can the leader be supported during this significant time of transition to play to their best.

The research has shown that investment in coaching can help leaders assimilate in the new role and accelerate the transition. Coaching at times of transition has strategic impact and value for both the leader and the wider organization.

Coaching in the context of a transition management relationship is but one solution and brings a unique and trusted relationship with the leader, which is ongoing over a number of months. The coach can get to know the leader's situation well and follows it as it changes. The development of new skills and behaviours will be geared to the specific needs of the unique time and circumstances in which the person leads.

The final word is that leaders have so much influence on the lives of others in organizations and the wider society. Equally, they will be influenced by so much around them. A coach's preparation for their work with leaders is a significant task, too. This book hopefully has signalled some of the steps the leader will take as they navigate their journey of leadership transition while also being a roadmap for coaches in their work.

Appendix

Framework of open-ended questions

1 Was this your first move into a leadership role?
Prompt: Have you had previous experiences of moving into leadership roles?

2 How long have you been in leadership roles overall?
Is it in the same organization or new organization? If in the same organization, have you moved to a new function/team?

3 Is this a role at a similar level or a higher level than your previous role?
Prompt: What is the overall size of the function / team that you lead (circa no. of employees)?

4 How did the coaching engagement come about?
Prompt: Who organized for the coaching to take place? At what stage after you moved to the role did the coaching commence? Was the coaching voluntary or mandatory? Who selected the coach? Have you been coached by this coach previously? Was the coach internal or external to the organization?

5 How did the process around working with the coach commence?
Prompt: Was there any contracting at the start of the coaching? What were the discussions like at the start? Was your manager involved in the process in any way? Or anyone else involved? Did you agree how often you would meet and where would you meet?

6 At the start, how did you experience working with the coach?
Prompt: What was it like for you in that space? What did you think the coaching would provide as you transitioned into the new role?

7 How would you describe the initial stages of the coaching?
Prompt: How were you experiencing it? What was the coaching bringing to the experience at the beginning, middle and towards the end?

8 What kind of things did the coaching address?
Prompt: How were these things decided upon? What do you perceive as your strengths? What about any areas for development? Were there opportunities you had at this time? Were there any challenges you faced? Did the coaching make a difference in any of these areas?

9 **What would you say was the impact of coaching for you as you transitioned into that new role?**

Prompt: Were there times or stages when the coaching had more impact for you? If so, can you tell me more about that?

10 **At what stage did the coaching cease or is it currently ongoing?**

Prompt: Has it finished? How many coaching sessions did you have overall? Are you likely to work with this coach again? Who finances the cost of the coaching? Is pre-approval elsewhere within the organization required for same?

11 **On a scale of 1 to 10 (with 1 as lowest value and 10 as highest value), where would rate the value you got from working with that coach at that time when you transitioned?**

Prompt: What was it bringing to you and how did you experience that? Was it taking anything away from you and how did you experience that?

12 **How do you think things changed for you?**

Prompt: What did you do differently? Would you recommend the use of a coach?

13 **If there was one word to describe the impact of working with that coach, what would it be?**

Prompt: If not a word, what phrase or sentence would you use to describe your experience to someone else?

14 **Is there anything you would like to add about your experience of working with a coach at that time?**

15 **Have you any concerns or queries at this stage that you would like me to address before we leave this interview?**

References

Allan, J. and Whybrow, A. (2008) Gestalt coaching. In S. Palmer and A. Whybrow (eds) *Handbook of Coaching Psychology: A Guide for Practitioners*. Hove: Routledge.

Beck, A.T. (1976) *Cognitive Therapy and the Emotional Disorders*. New York: Meridian.

Bentz, V.J. (1985) *A View from the Top: A Thirty-year Perspective on Research Devoted to Discovery, Description, and Prediction of Executive Behaviour*. Paper presented at the 93rd Annual Convention of the American Psychological Association, Los Angeles.

Berman, J. (2014) The three essential Warren Buffett quotes to live by. *Forbes*, 20 April 2014. Available at: https://www.forbes.com/sites/jamesberman/2014/04/20/the-three-essential-warren-buffett-quotes-to-live-by/#4f2b7c766543

Bond, A.S. and Naughton, N. (2011) The role of coaching in managing leadership transitions. *International Coaching Psychology Review*, 6(2): 165–179.

Bossert, R. (2005) New job? Go hire a transition coach. *Brandweek*, 46(5): 18.

Brann, A. (2014) *Neuroscience for Coaches: How to Use the Latest Insights for the Benefit of Your Clients*. London: Kogan Page.

Bridges, W. (2004) *Transitions: Making Sense of Life's Changes*, 2nd ed. Cambridge, MA: Da Capo Press.

Bridges, W. and Mitchell, S. (2000) Leading transition: A new model for change. *Leader to Leader*, 16(3): 30–36.

Bridges, W. and Mitchell, S. (2002) Leading transition: A new model for change. In F. Hesselbein and R. Johnson (eds) *On Leading Change*. San Francisco, CA: Jossey-Bass.

Burke, M. and Day, R.R. (1986) A cumulative study of the effectiveness of managerial training. *Journal of Applied Psychology*, 71(2): 232–245.

Campbell, D., Edgar, D. and Stonehouse, G. (2011) *Business Strategy: An Introduction*, 3rd ed. London: Palgrave Macmillan.

Charan, R., Drotter, S. and Noel, J. (2001) *The Leadership Pipeline*. San Francisco, CA: Jossey-Bass.

Chartered Institute of Personnel and Development (CIPD) (2014) *Leadership – Easier Said than Done*, Research Report, May. London: CIPD. Available at: https://www.cipd.co.uk/Images/leadership_2014-easier-said-than-done_tcm18-8893.pdf

Chartered Institute of Personnel and Development (CIPD) (2016) *HR Outlook: Leaders' Views of Our Profession*, Winter 2015–16. London: CIPD. Available at: https://www.cipd.co.uk/Images/hr-outlook_2016-winter-2015-16-leaders-views-of-our-profession_tcm18-11009.pdf

Ciampa, D. (2016) After the handshake. *Harvard Business Review*, 94(12): 60–68.

Coutu, D. and Kauffman, C. (2009) What can coaches do for you. *Harvard Business Review*, 87(1): 91–97.

Csoka, L.S. (1997) *Bridging the Leadership Gap*. New York: The Conference Board.

de Haan, E. (2008) I doubt therefore I coach: Critical moments in coaching practice. *Consulting Psychology Journal: Practice and Research*, 60(1): 91–105.

Dweck, C. (2016) *Mindset: The New Psychology of Success*, Revised ed. New York: Ballantine Books.

Ellis, A. (1962) *Reason and Emotion in Psychotherapy*. New York: Citadel Press.

Evers, W.J., Brouwers, A. and Tomic, W. (2006) A quasi-experimental study on management coaching effectiveness. *Consulting Psychology Journal: Practice and Research*, 58(3): 174–182.

Fong, G.T. and Markus, H. (1982) Self-schemas and judgments about others. *Social Cognition*, 1: 191–204.

Frankl, V.E. (1946/2008) *Man's Search for Meaning*. London: Ebury Publishing.

Gaffney, M. (2011) *Flourishing: How to Achieve a Deeper Sense of Wellbeing, Meaning and Purpose – Even When Facing Adversity*. Dublin: Penguin Ireland.

Gallwey, W.T. (2001) *The Inner Game of Work: Focus, Learning, Pleasure, and Mobility in the Workplace*. New York: Penguin Random House.

Gentry, W.A. and Chappelow, C. (2009) Managerial derailment: Weaknesses that can be fixed. In R.B. Kaiser (ed.) *The Perils of Accentuating the Positive*. Tulsa, OK: Hogan Press.

Goldsmith, M. and Reiter, M. (2013) *What Got You Here Won't Get You There: How Successful People Become Even More Successful*. London: Profile Books.

Goleman, D. (2000) Leadership that gets results. *Harvard Business Review*, 78(2): 78–90.

Gratton, L. (2010) The future of work. *Think*, 22 October 2010. Available at: www.london .edu/think/the-future-of-work

Gurdjian, P., Halbeisen, T. and Lane, K. (2014) Why leadership-development programs fail. *McKinsey Quarterly*, 1(1): 121–126.

Hogan, J., Hogan, R. and Kaiser, R.B. (2011) Management derailment. In S. Zedeck (ed.) *APA Handbook of Industrial and Organizational Psychology, Vol. 3. Maintaining, Expanding, and Contracting the Organization*. Washington, DC: American Psychological Association.

Johnson, G., Whittington, R. and Scholes, K. (2012) *Fundamentals of Strategy*. Upper Saddle River, NJ: Financial Times/Prentice Hall.

Kaiser, R.B. and Craig, S.B. (2011) Do the behaviours related to managerial effectiveness really change with organizational level? An empirical test. *The Psychologist-Manager Journal*, 14(2): 92–119.

Kaiser, R.B., Lindberg, J.T. and Craig, S.B. (2007) Assessing the flexibility of managers: A comparison of methods. *International Journal of Selection and Assessment*, 15(1): 40–55.

Kaplan, R.E. and Kaiser, R.B. (2006) *The Versatile Leader: Make the Most of Your Strengths – Without Overdoing It*. San Francisco, CA: Pfeiffer.

Keller, S. and Meaney, M. (2018) Successfully transitioning to new leadership roles. New York: McKinsey & Company. Available at: https://www.mckinsey.com/business-functions/organization/our-insights/successfully-transitioning-to-new-leadership-roles

Kihlstrom, J.F. and Klein, S.B. (1994) The self as a knowledge structure. In R.S. Wyer, Jr and T.K. Strull (eds) *Handbook of Social Cognition*. Hillsdale, NJ: Lawrence Erlbaum Associates.

Kovach, B.E. (1989) Successful derailment: What fast-trackers can learn while they are off the track. *Organizational Dynamics*, 18(2): 33–47.

Kuppler, T. (2015) Edgar Schein on culture. *Leadership and Change*. Available at: https://www.leadershipandchangemagazine.com/edgar-schein-on-culture/

Levin, I.M. (2010) New leader assimilation process: Accelerating new role-related transitions. *Consulting Psychology Journal: Practice and Research*, 62(1): 56–72.

Luthans, F. (2002) The need for and meaning of positive organisational behaviour. *Journal of Organisational Behaviour*, 23(6): 695–706.

Manderscheid, S. and Harrower, N.L. (2016) A qualitative study of leader transition and polarities. *Advances in Developing Human Resources*, 18(3): 390–408.

Mann, C. (2016) *Return on Investment*. 6th Ridler Report. London: Ridler & Co.

Markus, H. (1977) Self-schemata and processing information about the self. *Journal of Personality and Social Psychology*, 35(2): 63–78.

McCall, M.W., Jr. and Lombardo, M.M. (1983) *Off the Track: Why and How Successful Executives Get Derailed*. Technical Report No. 21. Greensboro, NC: Center for Creative Leadership.

Murphy, A. and Janeke, H.C. (2009) The relationship between thinking styles and emotional intelligence: An exploratory study. *South African Journal of Psychology*, 39(3): 357–375.

Neale, S., Spencer-Arnell, L. and Wilson, L. (2011) *Emotional Intelligence Coaching: Improving Performance for Leaders, Coaches and the Individual*. London: Kogan Page.

Neenan, M. and Dryden, W. (2000) *Essential Rational Emotive Behaviour Therapy*. London: Whurr.

Neenan, M. and Dryden, W. (2002) *Life Coaching: A Cognitive Behavioural Approach*. London: Brunner-Routledge.

Nelson, E. and Hogan, R. (2009) Coaching on the dark side. *International Coaching Psychology Review*, 4(1): 9–21.

Nin, A. (1961) *The Seduction of the Minotaur*. Chicago, IL: The Swallow Press.

Passmore, J. (ed.) (2010) *Excellence in Coaching: The Industry Guide to Best Practice*, 2nd ed. London: Kogan Page.

Pula, R.P. (1996) Alfred Korzybski, 1879–1950: A bio-methodological sketch. *Polish American Studies*, 53(2): 57–105.

Sedikides, C. (1993) Assessment, enhancement, and verification determinants of the self-evaluation process. *Journal of Personality and Social Psychology*, 65(2): 317–338.

Sejeli, D.S. and Mansor, N.A. (2015) Leadership derailment: Does self-leadership matter? *International Journal of Economics and Financial Issues*, 5: 22–26.

Seligman, M.E. (2012) *Flourish: A Visionary New Understanding of Happiness and Well-being*. Melbourne, Australia: Random House.

Seligman, M.E. and Csikszentmihalyi, M. (2000) Positive psychology: An introduction. *American Psychologist*, 55(1): 5–14.

Smith, C.L. (2015) How coaching helps leadership resilience: The leadership perspective. *International Coaching Psychology Review*, 10(1): 6–19.

Sy, T., Côté, S. and Saavedra, R. (2005) The contagious leader: Impact of the leader's mood on the mood of group members, group affective tone, and group processes. *Journal of Applied Psychology*, 90(2): 295–305.

Watkins, M. (2003) *The First 90 Days*. Cambridge, MA: Harvard Business School Press.

(2001) *The Business Coaching Revolution: Excellence through Partnership*. Dublin: Blackhall Publishing.

Weafer, S. (2001) *Excellence Through Partnership: The Business Coaching Revolution*. Dublin: Blackhall Publishing.

Wheeler, P. (2008) *Executive Transitions Market Study Report*. The Institute of Executive Development/Alexcel. Available at: https://www.slideshare.net/harv6pack/executivetransitionsmarketstudyreportpw

Whittington, J. (2016) *Systemic Coaching and Constellations: The Principles, Practices and Application for Individuals, Teams and Groups*. London: Kogan Page.

Wood, B. and Gordon, S. (2009) Linking MBS learning and leadership coaching. *International Coaching Psychology Review*, 4(1): 87–104.

Young, J.E., Klosko, J.S. and Weishaar, M.E. (2003) *Schema Therapy*. New York: Guilford Press.

Zaccaro, S.J. (2001) *The Nature of Executive Leadership*. Washington, DC: American Psychological Association.

Index